MAN ALIVE

An Unlikely Story in Three Acts

by
JOHN DIGHTON

LONDON
NEW YORK TORONTO SYDNEY HOLLYWOOD

Copyright © 1957 by John Dighton
All Rights Reserved

MAN ALIVE is fully protected under the copyright laws of the British Commonwealth, including Canada, the United States of America, and all other countries of the Copyright Union. All rights, including professional and amateur stage productions, recitation, lecturing, public reading, motion picture, radio broadcasting, television and the rights of translation into foreign languages are strictly reserved.

ISBN 978-0-573-01259-4

www.samuelfrench.co.uk
www.samuelfrench.com

FOR AMATEUR PRODUCTION ENQUIRIES

UNITED KINGDOM AND WORLD
EXCLUDING NORTH AMERICA
plays@samuelfrench.co.uk
020 7255 4302/01

Each title is subject to availability from Samuel French, depending upon country of performance.

CAUTION: Professional and amateur producers are hereby warned that *MAN ALIVE* is subject to a licensing fee. Publication of this play does not imply availability for performance. Both amateurs and professionals considering a production are strongly advised to apply to the appropriate agent before starting rehearsals, advertising, or booking a theatre. A licensing fee must be paid whether the title is presented for charity or gain and whether or not admission is charged.

No one shall make any changes in this title for the purpose of production. No part of this book may be reproduced, stored in a retrieval system, or transmitted in any form, by any means, now known or yet to be invented, including mechanical, electronic, photocopying, recording, videotaping, or otherwise, without the prior written permission of the publisher. No one shall upload this title, or part of this title, to any social media websites.

The right of John Dighton to be identified as author of this work has been asserted in accordance with Section 77 of the Copyright, Designs and Patents Act 1988.

MAN ALIVE

Produced at the Aldwych Theatre, London, on the 14th June, 1956, with the following cast of characters:

(in the order of their appearance)

WALDORF	*Brian Reece*
BELGRAVIA	*Joan Benham*
GEORGE INGLE	*David Evans*
DAPHNE JAMESON	*Wendy Craig*
MISS YATES	*Elizabeth Addyman*
OAKSHOTT	*Joan Hickson*
JUBILEE	*Joan Sims*
MR WEMBLEY	*Geoffrey Dunn*
MR HATHAWAY	*Robertson Hare*
THE DOORMAN	*Wilfred Boyle*
FRED	*Peter Retey*
MISS BUTTERWORTH	*Anna Barry*
MISS ADSHEAD	*Marjorie Dunkels*
THE POLICE COMMISSIONER	*Deering Wells*

Directed by WILLIAM CHAPPELL
Setting by HUTCHINSON SCOTT

SYNOPSIS OF SCENES

The action of the Play passes in a window of Hathaway's Stores in Oxford Street, London

ACT I
The morning of New Year's Day

ACT II
Half an hour later

ACT III
Half an hour later

Time—the present

ACT I

SCENE—*A "Bedroom" in Oxford Street, London. The morning of New Year's Day.*

The room, which is panelled and painted in a light pastel shade, is laid out enough, yet there is something conventionally strange about it. This is partly due, perhaps, to the absence of such normal architectural features as doors and fireplace, partly to the newness and careful arrangement of the furnishings, which conspire to give it a curiously unnatural air. Two curtained alcoves are set diagonally in the L and R back corners. In the alcove up L is a satin-covered double bed. In the alcove up R the end of a bathroom is visible, with a towel rail, and a cork-seated stool. A curtained arch C of the back wall leads to the various sales departments and other parts of the building. The glass front of the window, facing the street, is presumed to be along the footlights. The alcoves give access to other windows R and L. A batten, with a tasselled fringe, representing the bottom edge of the window blind, is suspended across the front of the stage at floor level, and can be raised or lowered at will. The handle or pulley for this is fixed to the wall down L. There is a dressing-table with mirror and stool against the wall R. A chaise-longue stands C with a small circular table above it. There are two upright chairs which normally stand R of the exit up C and against the wall L. A small table stands L of the exit up C with a table-lamp and a telephone on it. There are electric wall-brackets on the walls R and L and in the alcove up L. The alcove up R is lit by an electric globe pendant. The switches are behind the right pillar of the exit up C.

When the CURTAIN *rises, it is shortly before 9 a.m. The window "blind" is down, and the window is dimly lit. The occupants of the room, of which there are two, seem to have caught something of its artificiality. The figure of a woman,* BELGRAVIA, *elegant in a self-consciously draped housecoat, reclines on the chaise-longue, with a deadpan expression, reading a book. The figure of a man,* WALDORF, *stands stiffly down L, hands on hips, in a pair of new mauve pyjamas, a purple silk dressing-gown and blue bedroom slippers. He has his back to a streamlined sun-lamp which is focused obliquely on him, but which is not switched on.* WALDORF *and* BELGRAVIA *look about thirty years of age. Neither of them has a hair out of place. Both are motionless and, like the room, have what can best be described as an unlived-in look about them. The chair from R of the exit up C is behind the chaise with a boy's rather violent-coloured dressing-gown draped over it. After a few moments,* GEORGE INGLE *enters hurriedly up C. He is in his middle twenties, is rather matter-of-fact, and is neatly dressed in a dark suit. He carries a notepad and pencil and a cardboard box, all of which he puts on the bed. The occupants of the room remain motionless and* GEORGE *takes no more notice of them than he does of the furniture, rather less, in fact, for having removed his jacket in a business-like way, he moves to the entrance up* C, *switches on the lights, then returns to the cardboard box, opens it, and bends over it, sorting the contents.* DAPHNE JAMESON, *a pretty girl of twenty enters up* C. *She wears a plain dark dress, but life to her is full of romantic possibilities. Her manner is less hurried than George's. She carries a feather duster. She sees George, smiles, moves quietly behind him and puts her arms around his waist.* GEORGE *is mildly startled.*

GEORGE (*without looking round; with a grin*) Hullo, Daphne.
DAPHNE. 'Morning, George.

(GEORGE *continues with his sorting*)

(*In reproof*) George!

(GEORGE, *still in Daphne's arms, turns and they kiss.* DAPHNE *attempts to kiss him again*)

GEORGE (*mildly reproving*) Now, Daphne . . .
DAPHNE. No-one can see us. (*She kisses him*) We might be in our own home—in our own bedroom—(*with a little sigh*) if we ever have one. (*She sits on the end of the bed*)
GEORGE. If we both get the sack, we'll never afford even to get married. (*He attempts to break from her*) It's five to nine . . .
DAPHNE (*holding on to him; romantically*) Five to nine—on a Saturday evening—the moon is shining in at the window—we're very much in love. (*She pulls George on to the end of the bed and kisses him, rather over-passionately*)
GEORGE (*quite shocked*) Daphne! (*He looks guiltily around*)
DAPHNE (*still holding on to him; happily*) It's all right. (*She looks towards the audience*) The blind's down.
GEORGE (*a little anxiously*) That's just it—and if it's down much longer, there'll be hell's delight. (*He frees himself and rises*) Come on—I've got the list. You do that side and I'll do this. (*He glances at his notepad, gives Daphne a number of show cards and price tickets from the cardboard box, then takes some show cards and price tickets for himself and moves to Waldorf*)
DAPHNE. Every time I feel romantic, there's a reason not to.
GEORGE (*turning Waldorf to front*) Well, there's a time and a place for everything. (*He attaches one price ticket which reads "9 guineas" to the front of Waldorf's dressing-gown, and another ticket reading "59/3" to the pyjamas. He adjusts the clothing generally and rearranges Waldorf's arms*)

(WALDORF, *whose air of artificiality is now accounted for, naturally remains as motionless as ever*)

DAPHNE (*rising resignedly and moving below the downstage end of the chaise*) I know, and it isn't Saturday evening. It's Monday morning. (*With feeling*) I don't know who invented Sales, but I bet they never had to serve in one. (*She is about to put a show card on Belgravia, but pauses and reads it*) "What every Boy Wants"—that can't be right.
GEORGE (*indicating the boy's dressing-gown*) That's for *that*.
DAPHNE (*putting the card on the dressing-gown*) Did you see the paper this morning? Whole page advertisement. "Happy New Year. Hathaway's Can Supply It." That's all it said. (*Remembering*) Oh—"And At Half the Price". (*She selects another show card*) "Housewives' Choice." (*She moves above the chaise and moves Belgravia's hand*) I ask you. (*She puts the show card on Belgravia*) I suppose the old man's just discovered the Light Programme. And if it's really true he writes the ads, in addition to everything else, I think he's going crackers. (*She moves below the downstage end of the chaise*)
GEORGE (*putting a price ticket on the sun-lamp*) Probably New Year's Day coming slap on a Monday. Gone to his head a bit. (*He kneels and adjusts the angle of the lamp*)
DAPHNE (*after a pause; dreamily*) I had a funny feeling, when I woke up this morning. I suppose that's what it was.

(GEORGE, *still on his kness, stares enquiringly at* DAPHNE)

I always feel anything can happen on New Year's Day. (*She crosses to George and strokes his hair*)
GEORGE (*rising and crossing to the dressing-table*) It very likely will —if we don't get this blind up on the dot. (*He positions some price tickets and show cards on the dressing-table*) Old Wembley's in a filthy mood this morning. He always is, just before a Sale.
DAPHNE. So's Yates. But it isn't that—it's because she's had to share this window. She was planning to fill the whole thing with drastically reduced underwear.
GEORGE. I don't know why the old man's so keen on these mixed windows—bit of every department ... (*He gestures around, then moves to the table above the chaise and adjusts the position of the vase of flowers*) You've got to go surrealist nowadays. (*He crosses to Waldorf*) That's the only way to make 'em stop and look. (*He adjusts Waldorf's position a little*)
DAPHNE (*looking towards Waldorf*) Well, he looks a bit surrealist, if you ask me.
GEORGE (*proudly*) Not bad, is it? Gives the window *something*, anyway. (*He indicates the sun-lamp*) I found this in Electrical. Just in. The very last word. Double Strength U.V.
DAPHNE. You what?
GEORGE. Ultra violet, like the sun radiates. Very invigorating.
DAPHNE (*abstractedly*) Shall we go skating tonight?
GEORGE. What? (*He stands down* L *of Waldorf and looks at him*)

DAPHNE. Skating. (*She moves below the chaise, imitating skating*)
GEORGE (*incredulously*) Tonight? (*He adjusts Waldorf's head*) If I know anything about my feet, they'll have no desire to be on ice. (*He moves to the cardboard box on the bed*) They'll want to be in a mustard-bath. (*He takes two show cards from the box*) Yours, too, I should have thought. (*He moves to* R *of Waldorf and places the show card in Waldorf's hand. It reads* "*Ultra-Violet*")
DAPHNE (*sighing*) Oh, George—there are other things in life besides one's feet.
GEORGE. Not on the first day of a Sale. (*He puts another show card on the floor in front of Waldorf and the lamp. This, too, reads* "*Ultra-Violet*")
DAPHNE (*looking a little sadly at George*) You know such a lot about so many things.
GEORGE (*modestly*) Well, I try to keep learning.
DAPHNE. If only you knew a little more about life.
GEORGE. What's that got to do with going skating?
DAPHNE. Oh—(*she turns away*) you're hopeless. (*She turns to Belgravia, swivels her legs to the floor, then sits on the end of the chaise*)
GEORGE. Well, it's quite a reasonable question.
DAPHNE (*with spirit*) That's it. You always want to do what's reasonable. You won't even get married because we can't afford it.

(GEORGE *attempts to speak*)

If you had any life in you at all—(*she rises and crosses to George*) you'd say: "Let's get married and starve, what does it matter?"
GEORGE. There wouldn't be much life in either of us, then, would there?

(DAPHNE, *exasperated, is about to retort.*
MISS YATES *enters up* C. *She is in the early forties, efficient and well turned out, but with any femininity in her kept rigidly out of working hours.* DAPHNE *rises hurriedly and resumes work.* GEORGE *hastily does likewise*)

Good morning, Miss Yates.
DAPHNE (*replacing Belgravia's legs on the chaise; hastily*) We're nearly through, Miss Yates. (*She adjusts Belgravia's housecoat, then moves above the chaise*)
MISS YATES (*brusquely*) Good morning. (*She moves down* RC, *turns and surveys the window with a professional eye, then makes one or two small adjustments*) Yes—yes—the flowers ... (*She indicates the flowers on the table above the chaise. To Daphne*) A little further to the left.

(DAPHNE *moves the flowers back to the place from which George moved them.* GEORGE *notices but says nothing*)

That's better. (*She catches sight of Waldorf*) That's ridiculous ...

(GEORGE *turns Waldorf to face down* R)

(*She checks herself with some exasperation*) Oh well, I suppose it's not my business. (*She moves below the chaise and looks at Belgravia. Dubiously*) Mm—I suppose so. (*She looks at the boy's dressing-gown*) No. That I really can't have. It clashes horribly.

(GEORGE *bends and moves Waldorf's right leg*)

(*She turns to George*) I'm sorry, but you'll have to move it.

(GEORGE'S *seat only is presented to her*)

(*Sharply*) Mr Ingle!
    GEORGE (*straightening up and turning; innocently*) Yes, Miss Yates? Move what?
    MISS YATES. "What Every Boy Wants". It won't do there at all. (*She crosses to the dressing-table*)
    GEORGE. Oh. (*He surveys the window*) There's a bit of a gap here. I'll shift it. (*He points* C)
    MISS YATES. No, no—right out of the window.
    GEORGE (*after a pause*) But Mr Wembley said specially . . .
    MISS YATES. I can't help what Mr Wembley said.

(DAPHNE *idly dusts the flowers with a feather duster*)

GEORGE. He's got fifty-three of these dressing-gowns, left over from Christmas before last. They won't seem to go.
    MISS YATES. Well, this one's got to. Take it away at once.
    GEORGE (*giving up*) O.K. (*He moves to the dressing-gown, picks it up with the show card, places the chair* R *of the entrance up* C, *then turns to go*)
    MISS YATES. Mr Wembley has only himself to blame, if he buys unsaleable stock.
    DAPHNE (*mischievously*) What every boy doesn't want, apparently.
    MISS YATES (*severely*) Miss Jameson. (*To George*) And I'll fill the gap.
    GEORGE. Whatever you say, Miss Yates. Until Mr Wembley says something different.

(GEORGE *exits up* C. MISS YATES *looks exasperatedly after him for a moment, then turns to Daphne*)

MISS YATES. Just finish that, and I'll find you something. (*She moves to the head of the chaise*) We've plenty of obstinate lines of our own, that will really repay pushing.
    DAPHNE. Yes, Miss Yates.

(MISS YATES *looks at Belgravia*)

MISS YATES (*pulling Belgravia's head backwards*) This is a common old model—(*she pushes Belgravia's head back into position*) couldn't you find a better one?

DAPHNE. Nothing that would go on that chaise-longue thing.

MISS YATES (*resignedly*) Oh, well. (*She moves to the exit up* C) That housecoat would look good on anything—that's one comfort.

(MISS YATES *exits up* C.

DAPHNE *follows Miss Yates off. There is a moment's silence. Then, still otherwise motionless,* BELGRAVIA *speaks*)

BELGRAVIA. In my opinion, that woman is a first-class bitch.

(WALDORF *answers in the same motionless manner, but whereas Belgravia's tone is sophisticated, his is completely the reverse*)

WALDORF (*simply*) I don't know what that is.

BELGRAVIA. Don't worry—when you've been here a few months you'll be an expert. You're new, aren't you?

WALDORF. I was delivered on Saturday.

BELGRAVIA. I thought I hadn't seen you before. Though, of course, in an emporium of this size, one hardly even knows the dummies in the next window. Thank God.

WALDORF. Have you been here a long time?

BELGRAVIA. Long enough. If you're thinking of that Yates woman's remark, it was entirely uncalled for. Common old model, indeed. I'm not even chipped—anywhere. Though I say it myself, I come of a very good factory. A lot of my contemporaries went to Harrods and Marshalls and Harvey Nichols and really first-class shops like that. (*Resignedly*) Still, we can't choose our store in life and there it is. A fine day you elected to start. January Sale.

WALDORF. Is that bad?

BELGRAVIA. You have no idea. Two thousand women fighting to pay too much for what they afterwards discover they never wanted in the first place.

WALDORF (*with a gleam in his eye*) Two thousand women!

BELGRAVIA. Of course, the White Sale is even worse. Last year I was dressed entirely in lace table mats.

WALDORF. Table mats?

BELGRAVIA. It was draughty in the extreme. Normal people put them on tables. It took one of Mr Hathaway's happy inspirations to put them on me.

WALDORF. Do women come to the White Sale, too?

BELGRAVIA. Nothing else but.

WALDORF. I think I'm going to like it here.

BELGRAVIA. Whether you do or don't, what can women possibly have to do with it?

WALDORF. I don't know. I've only seen one or two. I like the look of them.

BELGRAVIA (*a little anxiously*) There isn't anything peculiar about you, is there?

ACT I   MAN ALIVE   7

WALDORF. Not that I know of.

(DAPHNE *enters up* C. *She carries a show card and a bed jacket. She moves the chair* R *of the exit up* C *and places it* LC)

BELGRAVIA. Believe me, when you've seen as many women as I have . . .

WALDORF (*with his eyes on Daphne*) Sssh! She'll hear you.

BELGRAVIA. Don't be ridiculous—she can't. Humans can't hear us.

(DAPHNE *evidently can't. She is busy with the bed jacket and show card on the chair*)

And when they look us in the eye *we* can't speak. So there's no contact. We're in two different worlds. Silly little thing, this one is.

(DAPHNE, *singing the first line of "Love is a many splendoured thing", moves to Belgravia and slightly adjusts her housecoat. During this,* BELGRAVIA *is mute.* DAPHNE *moves up* R *of Belgravia*)

See what I mean?

WALDORF. I wish I could speak to her.

BELGRAVIA. If you could, you'd give her the fright of her life. She talks the most arrant nonsense, anyway. Romance with a capital R. And she hasn't the first idea how to pose one. She had my hands on back to front one day last week. So busy dreaming about Life and George. (*She imitates Daphne's way of saying* "*George*")

(MISS YATES *enters up* C)

MISS YATES (*to Daphne*) Haven't you done it yet? (*She glances at her wrist-watch*) It's time this blind was up.

DAPHNE. I'm waiting for George. He's bringing it in.

BELGRAVIA (*to Waldorf*) See what I mean?

MISS YATES. Mr Hathaway will have quite enough on his mind this morning, without a delayed window. He'd be extremely angry. I don't want that, even if it is Mr Wembley's fault. (*She indicates the chair* LC) We could have that chair down here. (*She moves down* R)

(OAKSHOTT *enters up* C. *She is a severely dressed store detective, a militant ex-policewoman. She carries some items of women's clothing, a coat, cardigan, dress and hat. She is looking for Miss Yates*)

OAKSHOTT (*moving* C) Ah—Miss Yates . . .

MISS YATES (*exasperated*) Oakshott—since when has a window been the store detective's province?

BELGRAVIA. She's off her beat.

OAKSHOTT (*bristling at Miss Yates*) The extent of my province, Miss Yates, is not *your* province. (*She glares*) Happy New Year.

MISS YATES (*glaring*) Same to you, I'm sure.

OAKSHOTT. I've taken these items out of stock. (*She puts the hat on the chair* LC) No objection, I hope?
MISS YATES (*moving to* R *of Oakshott; formidably*) Taken them?
OAKSHOTT. *Borrowed* them. For the Sale. You know what these shoplifters are. If I don't camouflage myself thoroughly, they spot me in a jiffy and then there's nothing doing. Can't have that.
BELGRAVIA (*dryly*) Oh, no—mustn't discourage them.
OAKSHOTT. There is this cardigan at thirty-five and six, this dress and coat at five and seven guineas, and a hat from the six-and-elevenpenny counter.
BELGRAVIA. Expensive at the price.
MISS YATES. Very well. (*Snootily*) Just see they're returned in due course. (*She moves down* R) They'll have to go into "Shop Soiled". (*To Daphne*) Now, as I said before, we could have that chair down here... (*Ignoring Oakshott, she shows Daphne where to place the chair*)

(DAPHNE *picks up the chair* LC)

OAKSHOTT (*fuming*) Really—(*she grabs the hat from the chair*)

(DAPHNE *moves the chair down* R)

—sometimes I wish I were back in the Force. At least the sergeant never snubbed me when I drew my uniform.

(OAKSHOTT *exits up* C)

MISS YATES (*moving the chair immediately down* R *of the chaise*) That's right—now drape the bed jacket over it.

(DAPHNE *drapes the bed jacket over the chair.*
GEORGE *enters up* C. *He is carrying* JUBILEE, *his arms grasped round her middle. She is a girl child dummy, about twelve years of age in appearance, with a bright, fixed smile. She wears a party frock and has her hair in pigtails. Her manner of speaking is that of a rather over-bright woman in the late fifties*)

GEORGE. Here we are.
BELGRAVIA (*half to herself*) Oh, God—I might have guessed that.
JUBILEE. Happy New Year, everyone.
GEORGE (*moving* LC *with Jubilee*) About here, Miss Yates?
MISS YATES (*glancing up*) Yes—that'll do.

(GEORGE *places* JUBILEE LC *so that she half faces Belgravia*)

JUBILEE (*brightly*) Good morning, Belgravia.
BELGRAVIA (*sourly*) Morning.
JUBILEE. What are you reading, dear?
BELGRAVIA (*bitterly*) The Textile Trade Year Book for nineteen-twenty-six. Upside down.

(GEORGE, *dissatisfied with Jubilee's position, shifts her round, so that now she half faces Waldorf*)

JUBILEE (*to Waldorf*) I don't think we've met before.
WALDORF. No. I'm new.
JUBILEE. Straight here from the maker's, I hope?
WALDORF. I came out of the mould last week.
JUBILEE. Just at the start of life. How nice.

(GEORGE *turns Jubilee to face front but is dissatisfied and looks towards Miss Yates*)

GEORGE. I can't tell which way she looks best.
BELGRAVIA (*in an undertone*) Who could?
MISS YATES (*impatiently*) Never mind—we'll see to it.
GEORGE. I'll get the remainder.

(GEORGE *exits up* C)

MISS YATES (*crossing to Jubilee*) Have you got the card that goes with it?

(DAPHNE *crosses to Miss Yates and hands her a show card*)

(*She looks at the show card*) "Glamorous Nights". No—I really think not. (*Exasperatedly*) We'll have to find another one. (*She moves to the exit up* C) And quickly.
DAPHNE (*crossing and putting the feather duster on the end of the bed*) It's just on nine, Miss Yates.
MISS YATES (*impatiently*) Exactly. I've been pointing that out for the past ten minutes.

(MISS YATES *exits up* C.
DAPHNE *follows her off*)

JUBILEE (*brightly*) Well, this *is* a pleasant surprise. One of my favourite windows, too—Number Thirteen. I was so afraid I was going to miss the best of the Sale. I had a most disappointing position, tucked away in that horrid narrow passage outside the Tea Room.
BELGRAVIA (*dryly*) And the "Ladies".
JUBILEE. Well, yes. And people squeeze past so—especially at Sale Time. I was there once before, a year or two ago—and I was knocked over. Such crowds.
WALDORF (*with a gleam in his eye*) Crowds of women?
BELGRAVE. Those are what usually patronize the "Ladies".
JUBILEE. Of course, he's new to it all, isn't he? We must say "Welcome to Hathaways".
BELGRAVIA. Anybody's welcome to it.
JUBILEE. Oh, come now—it's a very good house. It may not be Debenhams or Selfridges, but it has something that they haven't . . .

BELGRAVIA (*dryly*) Mr Hathaway.
JUBILEE. The family tradition. After all, I was here with his father, *and* his grandfather and I know. The changes I've seen in my time . . .
BELGRAVIA (*familiar with them*) Horse buses in Oxford Street—hansom cabs—sedan chairs, probably.
JUBILEE (*reprovingly*) Now, Belgravia—you're teasing.
WALDORF. What does that mean—"Belgravia"?
BELGRAVIA. It doesn't mean anything. It's my name.
WALDORF. Name?
BELGRAVIA. Like Thingummy-jig or What-d'you-call-it.
JUBILEE. Of course. Every model has a name.
WALDORF. I haven't.
JUBILEE. Oh, yes, you have. You must have. The makers always put one on.
BELGRAVIA. They stamp it, rather impertinently, on one's behind. I suppose it's the only place, these days, that they can be reasonably certain will not be exposed to the public.
WALDORF. I wonder what my name is.
BELGRAVIA. "Waldorf". I saw it this morning, earlier on.
JUBILEE. When they were dressing the window, I expect.
BELGRAVIA. When they were dressing Waldorf.
JUBILEE. Oh, Belgravia!
WALDORF (*trying it out*) Waldorf. (*In a different tone*) Waldorf.
JUBILEE. My name is Jubilee. That's because I came out at the time of a royal anniversary.

   (GEORGE *enters up* C. *He carries a pale pink plastic squeaking duck*)

BELGRAVIA. Not George the Fifth's. either. Queen Victoria's.
JUBILEE. Yes. I'm fifty-nine this year.

   (GEORGE *moves to Jubilee and puts the duck in her arm*)

You wouldn't think it to look at me, would you?

   (GEORGE *moves down* R *of Jubilee and looks at her.*
      MR WEMBLEY *enters up* C *and moves down* L *of Jubilee. He is a fussy man in the early forties. His manner is pettish*)

WEMBLEY (*to George*) The doors are just opening. Why isn't this blind up?
GEORGE. Won't be half a minute, Mr Wembley.
WEMBLEY. You know what Mr Hathaway is. What's the delay?
GEORGE. Just waiting for a show card. Miss Yates is bringing it. (*He moves to the upstage end of the dressing-table and adjusts the items on it*)
WEMBLEY (*exasperated*) Miss Yates. (*He moves to the bed*) I don't know why it is, but some women can never be on time with anything. (*He pushes the bed further into the alcove*)

BELGRAVIA. I've always thought his mother must have been several months ahead—with him.

WEMBLEY (*to George*) I said not a word when we had to share the window—(*he tidies the corner of the bed cover*) but I knew perfectly well how it would be.

(MISS YATES *enters up* C. *She carries a fresh show card for Jubilee*)

(*He moves down* LC, *turns and stares at the chair and bed jacket*) Where's that dressing-gown from Boy's Outfitting?

MISS YATES. I had it taken out. (*She crosses to the dressing-table and puts the card on the stool*)

WEMBLEY (*turning angrily to Miss Yates*) Well, really! There are some things I *won't* put up with.

MISS YATES. It was quite impossible. (*She moves to the chair* RC *and fiddles with the bed jacket*) Hideous colour, poor quality . . .

WEMBLEY (*outraged*) It was a pure Kidderminster Cashmere.

MISS YATES (*disregarding this*) And it ruined the look of the window.

WEMBLEY (*seething*) Miss Yates—I've been dressing windows for over twenty years.

BELGRAVIA. She won't try to compete with that one.

MISS YATES. That's probably just the trouble. Years ago, any old thing would do. (*She crosses to* L *of Jubilee and rearranges the duck*) I'm not going to lose sales, through having a lot of distracting clutter. (*She indicates Waldorf and the sun-lamp*) I'm putting up with *that* as it is.

WEMBLEY (*sarcastically*) You'll surely allow me one or two items . . . (*He looks at Waldorf, then stares at the sun-lamp*) What's that?

GEORGE. It's a sun-lamp, Mr Wembley.

MISS YATES. That's what I'm speaking about.

GEORGE (*to Wembley; eagerly*) It's the latest kind of U.V. And it's got I.R., too. Infra Red. You can switch from one to the other.

WEMBLEY (*pettishly*) I gave no instructions for that. None at all.

GEORGE. Well, I thought it would be a sort of unusual touch.

(MISS YATES *moves above the right end of the chaise and adjusts the collar of Belgravia's housecoat*)

WEMBLEY. Unusually stupid, I should say. What's the point of it? What on earth's the point?

MISS YATES. The point would be obvious to a child of ten. It's to focus attention on the dressing-gown *and* the lamp.

GEORGE (*crossing to* R *of Wembley; eagerly*) That's what I thought Sort of surrealist. And both being ultra-violet—more or less . . .

WEMBLEY (*irritated*) Surrealist? What does that mean?

GEORGE (*stumped*) Well—I don't know exactly.

Miss Yates (*moving to the dressing-table; to Wembley*) As a matter of fact, it's the one original thing in your part of the window.

(George *moves down* L *to Waldorf*)

Wembley (*crossing to Miss Yates; angrily*) Well, I like that! Half a minute ago you were complaining about it . . .

Miss Yates (*maddeningly*) I said I'd put up with it. You can hardly call that complaining.

Wembley (*with rising heat*) Miss Yates—I don't know if you're trying deliberately to provoke me . . .

Miss Yates (*equally angry*) Really! You're quite impossible!

(Mr Hathaway *enters up* C *and moves down* C. *He is a well-groomed, well-fed man of about forty-five, self-assured to the point of pomposity. His appearance signalizes an immediate, shocked silence*)

Belgravia. Something tells me we are in the Presence.

Hathaway (*ominously*) Happy New Year to everyone.

Miss Yates ⎫
George   ⎬ (*together*) Happy New Year, Mr Hathaway.
Wembley   ⎭

Hathaway. It's two minutes past nine—on what is undoubtedly the most important shopping day of the year—and this window is not yet pulling its weight. May I ask why?

Jubilee. Straight to the point. That's Mr Hathaway for you.

Hathaway (*moving above the chaise*) You may well be ashamed to answer. You know perfectly well the importance I attach to our window displays. Upwards of forty thousand people pass these windows every hour. At sale time, probably more. There are eighteen windows in the frontage—(*he stands immediately above Belgravia*) not counting the back and sides——

Belgravia. Well, how *can* you, in the frontage?

Hathaway. —which means—(*he leans on Belgravia's shoulder and pushes her forward*) at a rough estimate, eighteen times forty thousand sales chances hourly. (*He pulls Belgravia back into place*) But *not* if we keep the blinds down. (*He moves down* C)

Wembley (*all humility*) I'm sure we're extremely sorry, Mr Hathaway.

Hathaway (*moving to Wembley*) An apology is not an explanation.

Miss Yates ⎫ (*simultaneously*) ⎧ Well, to start with . . .
Wembley   ⎭   ⎩ Miss Yates appears to think . . .

Hathaway (*silencing them with a gesture; disapprovingly*) Please remember the team spirit.

Belgravia. We must all pull together.

Hathaway. We must all pull together. (*He gives Wembley priority*) Wembley?

(MISS YATES *moves down* R. WEMBLEY *looks at Miss Yates then turns to Hathaway*)

WEMBLEY. Well, sir—it was only in the best interests of the house, of course—just a detail, really . . .

MISS YATES (*clear cut*) I objected to giving prominence in the window to an unsaleable line.

HATHAWAY (*with a step down stage; formidably*) An unsaleable line?

WEMBLEY (*hastily*) I'm afraid Miss Yates doesn't quite appreciate—she has rather less experience, after all . . . (*He glares at Miss Yates*) Naturally, as you know, sir, some lines take a little more moving than others . . .

HATHAWAY (*moving* L) Possibly. (*He turns*) They shouldn't.

WEMBLEY. Oh, quite, sir. (*He takes a step or two towards Hathaway*) But there it is. (*He eyes Jubilee's frock. Nastily*) If it comes to that, I seem to remember . . .

MISS YATES (*hurriedly*) It wasn't only the merchandise. As I pointed out to Mr Wembley, he already has more than his fair share of focus—(*she indicates Waldorf*) over there.

HATHAWAY. Over where?

BELGRAVIA. Now you're for it, Waldorf. Two minutes and you'll be outside the "Gentlemen's".

WEMBLEY (*agitatedly*) Miss Yates knows perfectly well I shall be changing that.

HATHAWAY. Changing what?

WEMBLEY. The sun-lamp, sir. (*With a nasty look at George*) For some reason I cannot fathom, my instructions were not totally adhered to this morning.

HATHAWAY (*nodding*) You mean it should be switched on, of course.

(WEMBLEY *looks startled*)

It's no use having an eye-catching device of that kind and then adopting half-measures.

WEMBLEY. Very true, Mr Hathaway. (*With a triumphant smile at Miss Yates*) Switched on, of course. (*He moves to* L *of Miss Yates*)

(GEORGE *switches on the lamp*. WALDORF *is suffused with ultraviolet light from the lamp*)

GEORGE. There we are, sir.

HATHAWAY. Excellent. What I should call a sort of surrealist effect. (*To Wembley*) What you were aiming at, of course.

(MISS YATES *turns away*)

WEMBLEY. Well, sir, I can't say I had exactly that term in mind. (*He eases his collar*)

(MISS YATES *laughs*)

But the general effect is what I imagined it might be.

HATHAWAY. I congratulate you. A very welcome piece of initiative and enterprise. (*He turns and looks at the lamp*)

(WEMBLEY *smiles uncomfortably*.

DAPHNE *enters precipitately up* C)

DAPHNE (*as she enters*) Oh, heavens, isn't this blasted blind up yet? (*She sees Hathaway. Aghast*) Oh—I'm so sorry . . .

HATHAWAY. Don't apologize, please. (*He looks at Wembley and Miss Yates and moves down* C) I'm glad to see one member of the staff with some thought for the shopping public. Wembley—please see this blind goes up without further delay.

(DAPHNE *moves* LC)

WEMBLEY (*chastened by Hathaway's tone*) Yes, Mr Hathaway.

HATHAWAY (*importantly*) And please remember—all of you—at Hathaway's, there is no such thing as an unsaleable line.

(HATHAWAY *exits with dignity up* C. *There is a momentary silence during which* WEMBLEY *and* MISS YATES *glare at each other*)

BELGRAVIA. You know, at times, I really find Mr Hathaway rather endearing.

(MISS YATES *picks up the show card from the stool and turns to Daphne*)

MISS YATES (*icily*) Miss Jameson—place this card, please. (*She moves* C *and holds out the card*)

(DAPHNE *moves to Miss Yates and takes the card*)

And then finish up.

(DAPHNE *moves to Jubilee*)

(*With a glance at Wembley*) If anyone should want me I shall be in Teen-age Underwear.

(MISS YATES *exits up* C)

BELGRAVIA. I can't see why anyone should—in Teen-age Underwear or anything else.

(DAPHNE *looks for a suitable place to put the card*)

JUBILEE. I wonder what that card says? (*In a pleased tone*) From here, it looks like "Rock-a-bye-Baby—two guineas".

(DAPHNE *puts the card at Jubilee's feet*)

BELGRAVIA (*dryly*) "Rock Bottom—two-and-six".

(DAPHNE *moves the duck. It squeaks*)

JUBILEE (*taken aback*) Oh! And they talk about inflation.
BELGRAVIA. Who cares? Personally, I never read my own publicity.

(WEMBLEY *looks in a pained manner at Waldorf and the lamp*)

GEORGE. Shall I get the blind up, Mr Wembley?
WEMBLEY (*crossing to* R *of Daphne; nastily*) I'm only waiting for Miss Yates' assistant to finish.
DAPHNE. I have.

(DAPHNE *exits up* C. WEMBLEY *nods to* GEORGE, *who moves to the blind pulley on the wall down* L)

WEMBLEY (*moving* LC; *acidly*) And when you've done that, perhaps you'll take a little of your initiative and enterprise to Cut-Price Cardigans. I anticipate a rush there.

(WEMBLEY *exits up* C)

BELGRAVIA (*dryly*) "Happy New Year. Hathaway's Can Supply It."

(GEORGE *operates the pulley. The fringed batten down stage slowly rises. The blue-ish white-ish light of day rises over the scene, climbing with the raising of the invisible blind, from floor to ceiling*)

JUBILEE. Ah, that's much better. I do like to look out.

(GEORGE *finishes and turns to look with satisfaction at Waldorf and the lamp. He has an idea, undoes the dressing-gown and opens it a little, so that the pyjamas show, too. He whistles softly to himself. He looks at the effect, is satisfied with it and moves up* C *towards the exit. He catches sight of Daphne's feather duster on the end of the bed. He retrieves the duster, and still whistling, casually dusts Waldorf, Jubilee and Belgravia during the next speech*)

BELGRAVIA. I can't think who likes to look in. What a nauseating domestic spectacle we present. Mother puts her feet up with a good book, dear little daughter clutches her disgusting duck, while father smugly limbers up with a sun-lamp, to gain the strength to raise an addition to the family.

(GEORGE *dusts the low cut neck of Belgravia's housecoat*)

And I'll thank you to keep that feather duster to yourself.

(GEORGE *collects his coat, the cardboard box with any remaining show cards and price tickets, and exits up* C)

WALDORF (*breathlessly*) Isn't it beautiful?
BELGRAVIA (*amused*) What! Oxford Street?
JUBILEE. Come, come—even *I* would hardly say that.

WALDORF. So many women. Beautiful!
BELGRAVIA. You know, you'll have to watch this. You seem to have some kind of an obsession.
WALDORF. So many—and all so different.
BELGRAVIA. All pretty much the same, believe me. You've only got to offer a woman the biggest monstrosity you have in stock and tell her it brings out the colour of her eyes and she'll fall for it every time.
WALDORF. She will?
BELGRAVIA. Certainly. They're all alike. Every time they stop and look in the window, I know exactly what they're going to say.
JUBILEE. They say some very rude things sometimes. And little boys write words on the window. Unfortunately, you can't shut your eyes to it.
BELGRAVIA. We all learn to lip-read, you know. You have to, out of sheer desperation. It seems even worse *not* to know what they're saying—until you do. Then you wish you hadn't.
JUBILEE. There were two able seamen, just before Christmas, when I was modelling a middy blouse. One of them asked the other what use I'd be in the Navy, and his reply was something I can't repeat in a mixed window. (*She pauses. Coyly*) But I could just hint at it, if you like. (*To Waldorf. Sharply and severely*) Young man! You should speak, when you're spoken to.
WALDORF (*vaguely*) I didn't hear you. It's the banging.
BELGRAVIA. What banging?
WALDORF. In my ears. It's been getting louder and louder. (*Rhythmically*) *Bang* bang, *bang* bang . . .

(*The sound of amplified heart-beats is heard*)

JUBILEE. *I* can't hear anything.
BELGRAVIA. Banging in the ears? Don't be ridiculous, only humans have that. It's their heart-beats or something.
WALDORF. And then there's the heat, too.
JUBILEE. Heat? It's freezing today.
WALDORF. It seems to be spreading all the time—right from the very middle.
BELGRAVIA. The middle of where?
WALDORF. The middle of me. Upwards and downwards and outwards.
BELGRAVIA. It's that sun-lamp. He said it was double-strength. I shouldn't be a bit surprised if you were just a pool of plastic by the end of the day.
JUBILEE. If he is, it'll ruin the dressing-gown and pyjamas.
WALDORF. It's along my arms and my legs . . .
BELGRAVIA. Pins and needles, they call that.
JUBILEE. Talking of haberdashery, I hear they're enlarging the

department. Of course in my time there was a place for everything and everything was in its place . . .

(WALDORF *moves slightly up and down on his toes*)

WALDORF (*with rising force*) Bang bang, bang bang—louder, louder, louder. (*He drops the show card from his hand*)
JUBILEE (*annoyed*) Well, really!

(DAPHNE *enters hurriedly up* C. *Her manner is a little fussed. She moves to the bed, looks for the dusting brush, cannot find it, so looks in other parts of the window*)

BELGRAVIA. If it's your dusting-brush, you silly girl, George took it. (*She imitates Daphne's tone when she says "George"*)
WALDORF. Louder—and louder—and *louder*—and LOUDER. (*On the last of these, he is almost shouting. He ends abruptly*)

(*The heart-beat sound ceases and a continuous oscillating noise, the transition sound, is heard.* DAPHNE, *unable to find the brush, finally gives up, shrugs cheerfully and is about to go when she notices that Waldorf's dressing-gown is undone. She moves to Waldorf and ties the cord of the dressing-gown, humming cheerfully to herself as she does so*)

DAPHNE (*to Waldorf*) There you are, Gorgeous. (*She smiles at him and pats his face*)

(WALDORF *suddenly kisses* DAPHNE, *who lets out a squeak of utter astonishment. The transition sound ceases*)

Oh! Who did that? (*She runs behind one of the curtains of the alcove up* L *and peeps out*)
JUBILEE (*to Belgravia*) My dear, you're right—he's melting.
BELGRAVIA. Melting my eye.

(DAPHNE *recovers and moves to* R *of Waldorf*)

DAPHNE (*angrily*) Who are you? How dare you?

(WALDORF *looks in surprise at Daphne*)

(*Outraged*) You kissed me! What are you doing in the window?
WALDORF (*staring wonderingly at her*) Something happened—you said "There you are, Gorgeous"—and then . . . (*He takes a stiff pace forward to her*)
DAPHNE (*staring at Waldorf and realizing what he is*) Oh—oh—oh! (*She runs wildly to the exit up* C *and calls*) George . . .

(DAPHNE, *wailing, runs out up* C. WALDORF *endeavours to follow her. He takes a stiff step or two, then stops, bewildered*)

WALDORF (*dazedly*) Something's happened to me. (*He takes another pace*)
BELGRAVIA. You're telling us!

WALDORF (*moving to Jubilee*) What is it? What's happened? (*He turns to Belgravia*) Belgravia—why don't you say something?

(BELGRAVIA *is motionless*)

JUBILEE. He can't even hear us any more.

WALDORF (*turning to Jubilee*) Jubilee—can't you hear me?

BELGRAVIA. If you ask me, he's turned human. That's what's happened to him.

(WALDORF *turns away from Jubilee, more and more bewildered*)

JUBILEE. Belgravia—don't be morbid!

(WALDORF *moves above the chaise*)

BELGRAVIA. Well, how else can you explain it? Look at him.

WALDORF. I spoke to the human and she heard me! I can move! (*He tries out various movements*) I can move everything. (*He moves down* R, *his bewilderment beginning to turn to delight*)

JUBILEE. He didn't look a defective model, either, but you never can tell, can you?

WALDORF. And I kissed her! I kissed her! She tasted delicious. (*He moves down stage until he "bumps" into the "glass" of the window*) I'm free! I'm as free as they are! The whole world's outside! (*He moves* L, *feeling the "window glass"*) What shall I do next? (*He moves* C) Where shall I go?

JUBILEE. You'll go straight back to the factory, that's what'll happen to you.

WALDORF. I can go anywhere! I can do anything!

BELGRAVIA. There'll be hell let loose in a minute, that's quite certain.

WALDORF. Two thousand women! Perhaps I can kiss them all! (*He starts delightedly for the exit up* C, *but freezes in his tracks, close by his original position near the sun-lamp as* . . .)

(GEORGE *enters belligerently up* C, *followed by* WEMBLEY, *armed with a feather duster; a very large uniformed* DOORMAN *with "Hathaway's" on his cap;* FRED, *a young handyman in a fawn alpaca coat;* MISS YATES *and* DAPHNE)

GEORGE (*as he enters*) Now then, what the blazes . . . ? (*He pulls up and looks blankly around*)

WEMBLEY. All right, Ingle—leave this to us.

(*They all pull up blankly.* GEORGE *stands* C *with* WEMBLEY L *of him. The* DOORMAN *stands up* R *of Waldorf and* FRED *above Waldorf.* MISS YATES *goes down* R. DAPHNE *stands* L *of Wembley*)

GEORGE. There's no-one here.

ACT I MAN ALIVE

MISS YATES. Of course there isn't—I never heard anything so ridiculous.
DAPHNE (*still agitated*) There was. I know there was. (*She sees Waldorf. In alarm*) There it is. (*She moves quickly behind Wembley*) It's still there.
GEORGE. Where?
DAPHNE. There. By the lamp.
DOORMAN. That's one of the dummies.
MISS YATES. Of course it is.
DAPHNE. I don't care. Whatever it is, it kissed me.
GEORGE. Now, Daphne . . .
DAPHNE (*agitated*) George—I tell you it did. Go and see for yourself.
GEORGE (*shrugging*) O.K. (*He moves towards Waldorf*)

(HATHAWAY *enters up* C *and moves down* LC. *He is steaming with indignation*)

HATHAWAY. What in the name of heaven . . . ?

(GEORGE *stops and turns*)

(*Outraged*) Wembley! All of you! Miss Yates! What's going on here?
MISS YATES. It's nothing at all, Mr Hathaway.
HATHAWAY. Nothing! Every rule of the house flouted. The Sale in full swing and bedlam in one of our best windows. (*He looks out front*) Look at all those idiots staring. (*He pushes Wembley towards the blind pulley. Agitated*) Get out of the window, or get the blind down.
WEMBLEY (*sharply*) Ingle! The blind!
GEORGE. Yes, Mr Wembley. (*He hurries to the blind pulley and lets it down with a run*)

(*The fringed batten quickly falls. The daylight is sharply excluded from the ceiling down to the floor*)

HATHAWAY (*impatiently and angrily*) Now then—what is all this? I want an immediate explanation.
DAPHNE (*agitatedly*) I'm sorry, Mr Hathaway—I couldn't help it—it was such a shock . . .
MISS YATES. Miss Jameson—pull yourself together.
WEMBLEY (*to Hathaway*) Just a lot of nonsense, sir, the girl's gone off her head.
GEORGE (*indignantly*) Daphne wouldn't say a thing if she didn't think something . . .
HATHAWAY (*interrupting*) Silence!

(*There is silence*)

(*To Daphne*) What shock? Couldn't help what?

DAPHNE. When he kissed me—(*she looks at Wembley*) I was so surprised...
HATHAWAY (*severely*) Wembley!

(WEMBLEY *reacts indignantly*)

MISS YATES (*to Hathaway*) She's just imagining things—she thought someone kissed her.
HATHAWAY (*outraged*) What! In the window?
MISS YATES. Of course it was nothing of the kind.
DAPHNE. He did. Over there—(*she moves up* R *of Hathaway*) in the pyjamas and dressing-gown.
MISS YATES. It's nervous overstrain, that's all it is—the first day of the Sale.
HATHAWAY. Obviously. The girl's hysterical.
DAPHNE (*hysterically*) I am *not* hysterical.
WEMBLEY. Don't argue with Mr Hathaway—he knows best.
HATHAWAY. She'd better go up to Sister and lie down.
MISS YATES. Yes, Mr Hathaway.

(MISS YATES *leads* DAPHNE *towards the exit up* C)

HATHAWAY (*moving down* R) But not for too long. We need everyone at the counters.

(DAPHNE *and* MISS YATES *exit. There is a general move towards the exit up* C)

(*To George. Sharply*) Not you. We shall want the blind up again.

(GEORGE *moves to the blind pulley*)

Wembley—is the window in order?
WEMBLEY (*taking a hasty look around*) Yes, Mr Hathaway. (*To George*) Just one moment. (*He hurriedly dusts the faces of Belgravia, Jubilee and Waldorf with the feather duster*)
BELGRAVIA. Not again!

(WEMBLEY *completes the dusting and moves hurriedly to join Fred and the Doorman near the exit up* C)

HATHAWAY (*icily*) Thank you. I trust the small matter of our January Sale can now proceed without any further disturbance. (*He moves towards the exit up* C)

(WALDORF *suddenly gives vent to a resounding sneeze. The others all freeze in their tracks, then, as of one accord, they turn and stare in the direction of the sound, astonishment on their faces.* WALDORF *gapes anxiously back at them*)

BELGRAVIA. Bless you.

(WALDORF *moves towards the exit up* C. *The others all move towards* WALDORF, *who suddenly changes direction.* GEORGE, *the* DOORMAN,

ACT I MAN ALIVE 21

WEMBLEY *and* FRED *plunge at Waldorf.* WALDORF *makes a dash below the chaise, bumping into* JUBILEE, *who bends over the chaise.* WALDORF *dodges round the chaise and exits up* C. *The* DOORMAN *follows below the chaise, followed by* WEMBLEY, HATHAWAY *and* FRED. HATHAWAY, *half way round, turns back to go to the telephone and collides with* FRED.
The DOORMAN, FRED *and* GEORGE *run off up* C. HATHAWAY *moves to the telephone and lifts the receiver*)

HATHAWAY (*into the telephone*) Nine-nine-nine... (*To Wembley*) Get the blind up——

(WEMBLEY *crosses quickly to the blind pulley*)

—no, down—oh, up—no, down.

(WEMBLEY *winds the blind twice up and down.* HATHAWAY *discovers the telephone is a dummy with only about eighteen inches of cord, and the two parts not even attached.*

WALDORF *runs on through the alcove up* R, *followed by the* DOORMAN, GEORGE *and* FRED. WALDORF *runs to the alcove up* L, *the others following. All three grab Waldorf and end in a heap on the bed*)

GEORGE (*triumphantly*) Got him!
WEMBLEY (*agitatedly*) Are you sure?
DOORMAN (*breathlessly*) We've got him O.K.
WEMBLEY (*fussily*) Are you all right, Mr Hathaway?
HATHAWAY (*impatiently*) Yes, yes—of course I am.
BELGRAVIA. Waldorf, I suppose, is merely in pieces.

(GEORGE *and the* DOORMAN, *holding* WALDORF *by the arms, bring him down* LC. FRED *moves to the exit up* C)

WEMBLEY (*vexedly*) Look at that spread—retails at fourteen guineas. (*He tries to smooth the bedspread, glancing nervously at Waldorf*)
HATHAWAY (*moving down* C; *anxiously*) Don't let go of him. Keep him there.
GEORGE (*indignantly*) He had a nerve! Kissing Daphne.
HATHAWAY (*impatiently*) Never mind the minor details——

(GEORGE *looks affronted*)

—he had the impertinence to steal the clothes off a dummy—in broad daylight. (*He moves to* R *of Waldorf*) I'm surprised at you.
WALDORF (*with a friendly smile*) I'm surprised, too.
JUBILEE. We're all surprised.

(WEMBLEY *moves to* R *of Hathaway*)

DOORMAN (*to Hathaway*) Where shall we take him, sir—to the staff office?

HATHAWAY. Like that? Through the departments? Have you thought for a moment what's behind there?
WEMBLEY (*nodding*) Corsets.
HATHAWAY. Exactly. We can hardly walk a man in pyjamas through there.
BELGRAVIA. Shake them to their foundations.
HATHAWAY. He'll have to stay here till he's dressed. (*To Waldorf*) Where are your clothes? (*To George and the Doorman*) Are they on underneath?

(GEORGE *and the* DOORMAN *raise the neck of Waldorf's pyjama jacket and look underneath*)

GEORGE (*shaking his head*) Only him, sir.
WALDORF (*with a friendly smile at Hathaway*) Only me.
HATHAWAY (*sharply*) Well, what have you done with them? Come along now.

(WALDORF *obediently takes a step towards Hathaway, but is restrained by George and the Doorman.* HATHAWAY *backs away and bumps into* JUBILEE, *who flops on to the chaise*)

(*Even more sharply*) Stay where you are. Don't you dare move.

(WALDORF *subsides*)

Doorman, is Oakshott on duty?
DOORMAN. Oh, yes, sir—should be.
HATHAWAY (*crossing and standing near the lamp*) Find her and tell her to come here at once—and then get back to work.
DOORMAN. Very good, sir.

(*The* DOORMAN *exits up* C)

BELGRAVIA. It'll take more than a store detective to sort this one out.
HATHAWAY (*to Waldorf*) Perhaps you'll be a little more co-operative when you're given in charge. You won't help yourself in the least by refusing to talk. Now—are you going to use your tongue, or aren't you?

(WALDORF *dutifully sticks his tongue out.*
MISS YATES *enters up* C *and moves down* RC)

(*He bristles with anger*) Oh! Impertinence! (*Impatiently*) Wembley, see if his things are in here somewhere.

(WEMBLEY *nods and searches around the window.* MISS YATES *stares at Waldorf*)

GEORGE (*tentatively*) Excuse me, sir.
HATHAWAY (*impatiently*) Yes, what is it?
GEORGE (*indicating the lamp*) If you go on standing there, you'll get sunstroke.

HATHAWAY. What? Oh, well, switch it off, can't you?
(WALDORF *pulls out Hathaway's tie.* HATHAWAY *angrily slaps Waldorf's hand.* WEMBLEY *searches around the bed*)
(*To Miss Yates, indicating Jubilee and Belgravia*) And you'd better move these—display them somewhere else for the time being. They only add to the confusion.
(WALDORF *hooks one of his own price tags on Hathaway's back*)
MISS YATES (*annoyed*) Very well, Mr Hathaway. (*She moves to Belgravia, straightens her, then moves to Jubilee and straightens her*)
(WALDORF *moves towards Miss Yates, but is restrained by* HATHAWAY. GEORGE *switches off the lamp.* FRED *goes to Jubilee and grasps her round the middle*)
JUBILEE. Oh, dear—back to I know where.
(FRED *carries* JUBILEE *out up* C)
MISS YATES (*picking up the duck and display card*) Let me see—what's in the next window?
WEMBLEY (*still searching*) Hardware in Twelve—(*he nods* R) Indoor Games in Fourteen. (*He nods* L)
MISS YATES. Indoor Games—she might go in with those.
BELGRAVIA. Well, really!
WEMBLEY. There isn't an inch of space. And, of course, Hardware is out of the question. (*He smiles nastily at Miss Yates and continues his search*)
HATHAWAY (*pacing above the chaise; with an air of inspiration*) I'm not so sure—what stock are they showing?
WEMBLEY (*to George*) What's the stock in Twelve?
GEORGE. Saucepans, Mr Wembley. Forty-eight different sizes. (*He moves to the chair* RC *and moves it up* RC)
(WALDORF *moves to the chair* L, *pulls it a little from the wall and practises sitting down*)
HATHAWAY (*after a pause; decisively*) Put her in there.
BELGRAVIA (*appalled*) With forty-eight saucepans?
HATHAWAY. Might make an effective contrast.
BELGRAVIA. Well, thanks for that small thought, anyway.
(GEORGE *moves to the chaise.* WALDORF *moves down* L, *peeps round the edge of the "blind" looks out front, and waves to imaginary women*)
MISS YATES. Thank you, Mr Hathaway. (*She smiles triumphantly at Wembley and moves to the chaise*)
HATHAWAY (*to George*) And when you've done that, go through all the fitting rooms—see if he changed in one of those.
GEORGE. Yes, sir.
MISS YATES (*nodding* R) Will she go in?

GEORGE Just about. We may have to move a few lids.

(MISS YATES *and* GEORGE *propel the chaise towards the alcove up* R)

BELGRAVIA (*as she goes*) Oh, well, it's all experience, I suppose. I've been almost everything *but* the kitchen stove.

(GEORGE *and* MISS YATES *exit with* BELGRAVIA *on the chaise, through the alcove up* R)

WEMBLEY (*moving to* L *of Hathaway*) I've searched high and low, Mr Hathaway.
HATHAWAY. Nothing?
WEMBLEY. Nothing, sir.
HATHAWAY. Well, he must have discarded them somewhere. (*He sees Waldorf at the "blind". Severely*) Come away from there. (*He crosses to Waldorf, leads him to the chair* L *and sits him in it*) Now, listen to me . . .

(OAKSHOTT *enters up* C. *She is now dressed as a typical Sale shopper, in the garments she brought in earlier on, and is complete with a handbag and a carrier bag with "Hathaway's" on it. She crosses to* R *of Hathaway and looks over his shoulder at Waldorf*)

(*He looks up exasperatedly and endeavours to keep his temper*) I'm sorry, madam, this is not one of the departments. (*He bundles Oakshott towards the exit up* C)
WEMBLEY (*intercepting Hathway*) It's Oakshott, sir.
HATHAWAY (*taken aback*) Oh. Is it? (*He glares at Wembley*)
OAKSHOTT (*brisk, efficient and cheerful*) Morning, sir. Beg pardon for the deception. (*She indicates her clothes*) New outfit for the Sale. Have to keep changing your turn-out. (*She puts her carrier bag under the table* C) Well, if I fooled you, sir, I should be able to fool a few of—(*she smiles heartily at Hathaway*) the criminal classes.

(HATHAWAY *is not amused and indicates Waldorf*)

(*With a professional air*) Now then, let's see what we have here. (*She crosses to Waldorf and peers at him*)
WALDORF (*looking up at Oakshott*) Beautiful!
OAKSHOTT (*sharply*) That'll do.

(HATHAWAY *moves down* C)

No use shamming delirious with me. Come along, now—on your feet. (*With an expert movement, she jerks Waldorf to his feet*)
WALDORF (*with a friendly smile*) Thank you very much.
OAKSHOTT (*looking very closely at Waldorf; to Hathaway*) New one, sir. Not one of my regulars.

(WALDORF *attempts to stroke* OAKSHOTT's *face, but she moves away abruptly*)

WEMBLEY. I just can't think how he got in the window, I can't, really.

(OAKSHOTT *takes a notebook and pencil from her bag.* WALDORF *peers curiously into the bag.* OAKSHOTT *snaps the bag closed, nearly catching his nose*)

OAKSHOTT. My experience of shop-lifters, they can get up to anything.

WEMBLEY. You can hardly call *him* a shop-lifter.

HATHAWAY (*impatiently*) Never mind what we call him, the point is he's dressed from head to foot in our stock. (*Sarcastically*) Or do you suggest those are his own things he's wearing?

(OAKSHOTT *looks at the label in the back of Waldorf's collar, then turns away a step or two and writes in her notebook.* WALDORF *takes Oakshott's collar to look down and drags her back*)

WEMBLEY. Oh, no, Mr Hathaway—(*he moves to* R *of Hathaway*) certainly not. (*To Oakshott*) That's one of our silk twill gowns at nine guineas and a pair of our best poplin slumber-wear at fifty-nine and three—or rather sixty-five and nine, with the frogging.

(OAKSHOTT *inspects the front of Waldorf's pyjamas for frogging*)

HATHAWAY (*irritated*) Oh, a fig for the frogging!

(WALDORF *touches Oakshott's dress in imitation of her action*)

OAKSHOTT (*to Waldorf*) Steady! Now, did you purchase these articles, and if so, can you produce a receipt?

WALDORF. No—no. (*His manner is amiably co-operative and quite unafraid*)

OAKSHOTT. Then how do you come to be wearing them?

WALDORF (*indicating Wembley*) He put me into them.

WEMBLEY (*indignantly*) I did nothing of the kind.

HATHAWAY (*dryly*) It seems a little unlikely.

OAKSHOTT (*to Hathaway*) You know what they are, sir. They often say they were just trying something on.

WEMBLEY (*still fuming*) Trying something on is certainly the word.

HATHAWAY. Wembley, please. There's no reason to get excited.

OAKSHOTT (*to Waldorf*) Name?

WALDORF. Waldorf, so they tell me.

OAKSHOTT (*writing*) Waldorf. Is that your first name or your last?

WALDORF. The very first—as far as I know.

OAKSHOTT. Surname?

(WALDORF *looks blankly at her*)

You refuse to give it?
WALDORF. I haven't got it to give.
HATHAWAY. Nonsense—you must belong to a family of some sort.
WALDORF. Oh, yes. (*To Oakshott*) I belong to Mr Hathaway's family. (*He smiles in a friendly way at Hathaway*)
HATHAWAY (*furiously*) He does nothing of the sort.

(WEMBLEY *stares in a puzzled way at Waldorf*)

OAKSHOTT (*cheerfully*) They'll try anything, sir, some of them.
WEMBLEY. You know, his face seems vaguely familiar . . .
HATHAWAY (*outraged*) Wembley!
WEMBLEY (*aghast*) Oh, I didn't mean that, sir. That's not what I meant at all—I meant . . .
HATHAWAY (*irritably*) Yes, well, never mind what you meant. Don't stand here—go and see if that boy's unearthed anything.
WEMBLEY (*hastily*) Yes, Mr Hathaway.

(WEMBLEY *exits hurriedly up* C)

OAKSHOTT (*writing in her notebook*) "Waldorf Hathaway."
HATHAWAY. *Certainly not!*
OAKSHOTT. I must just put what he says, sir. For the record. (*To Waldorf*) Of what address?
WALDORF. Hathaway's. Oxford Street, W.1.
HATHAWAY (*fuming*) Really! This is quite preposterous! (*He moves up* C)
OAKSHOTT (*unruffled*) Just let him run on, sir. It'll all come to light in court.
HATHAWAY (*moving down* C) That's exactly what I'm thinking of. I'd much sooner it came to light here and now. Sale time, the very last thing we can do with is the wrong kind of publicity. (*He moves* RC)
OAKSHOTT (*to Waldorf*) Do you persist in the correctness of these particulars?
WALDORF. Oh, yes. They're quite correct, thank you.

(OAKSHOTT *crosses below Waldorf and stands down* L *of him*)

HATHAWAY (*moving* C; *sarcastically*) I take it the proof of that will be found in your other clothes?
WALDORF. I have no other clothes.

(HATHAWAY *and* OAKSHOTT *stare at Waldorf*)

HATHAWAY (*exasperated*) Nonsense!

(GEORGE *dashes in up* C. *He carries a suit and other items of clothing*)

GEORGE (*moving to up* L *of Hathaway; triumphantly*) I found them, sir—in one of the fitting rooms.
HATHAWAY (*also triumphant*) Ah! (*To Waldorf*) Now what have you got to say?

(WEMBLEY *dashes in up* C)

WEMBLEY (*moving to George; agitatedly*) Ingle! Give those back at once. (*He grabs the clothes*)
HATHAWAY. What?
WEMBLEY. They belong to one of the customers.

(WEMBLEY *exits up* C. HATHAWAY *glares at George*)

GEORGE. In that case, sir—there's nothing at all.
HATHAWAY. There must be.

(WEMBLEY *enters up* C)

GEORGE (*shaking his head*) I've looked in all the others.
WEMBLEY (*moving to* L *of Hathaway; nodding*) Seems to be so, Mr Hathaway. Not a sign of anything.
HATHAWAY (*exasperated*) Well, for heaven's sake, they must be somewhere. Dammit, he can't have come in the nude.
WALDORF (*helpfully*) No, I came in the van.
HATHAWAY. Dressed like that, I suppose?
WALDORF. No. Not dressed at all.
OAKSHOTT (*to Hathaway*) Plea of absent-mindedness. I've known them try it before.
HATHAWAY (*to Waldorf; with rising anger*) So you arrived here in a van—with nothing on—and Wembley put you into those?
WALDORF. Yes—that's right.
HATHAWAY (*crossing to* R *of Waldorf*) In that case, you can hardly claim, can you, to be a genuine customer?
WALDORF. No. I'm a genuine dummy.
HATHAWAY. A what!
WEMBLEY. Well, really!
OAKSHOTT (*laughing*) That's a new one, sir—even to me. Like to hear the magistrates on that one. (*She laughs heartily*)
HATHAWAY (*angrily*) Oakshott!
OAKSHOTT (*pulling herself together*) Sir!
HATHAWAY. This is not being conducted for your amusement.

(WALDORF *copies Oakshott's laugh*)

(*To Waldorf*) Or yours. (*To Oakshott*) I want him dressed and out of here within the next ten minutes. He's taking up valuable window space. (*He crosses to* RC)
OAKSHOTT. Yes, sir—but if they can't find his clothes . . . ?

HATHAWAY. We shall have to provide some. See to that, Wembley, will you? (*He moves towards the exit up* C)
WEMBLEY (*shocked*) What, sir—out of stock?
HATHAWAY (*stopping and turning; impatiently*) Better that, than waste any more time. (*He turns to go*)
WEMBLEY (*fussily*) But how shall I charge them?
HATHAWAY (*exasperated*) Charge them to "out of pocket". (*Bitterly*) We shall be, anyway. And *hurry*.
WEMBLEY (*hastily*) Yes, Mr Hathaway.

(WEMBLEY *nods to George to help him, whips a tape measure out of his pocket, crosses to Waldorf and takes his measurements.* GEORGE *takes a paper and pencil from his pocket and crosses to* L *of Waldorf*)

HATHAWAY (*with vexation*) Heaven knows what's happening in the Sale. All this time, I should have had my finger on the pulse of events. (*He turns to go*)

(MISS YATES *enters through the alcove up* R *and moves to* R *of Hathaway*)

MISS YATES (*urgently*) Mr Hathaway . . .
HATHAWAY (*utterly exasperated*) Oh, what is it now?
MISS YATES. It's Mr Cosgrove of Hardware. He says he won't have that model in his window—he'd sooner resign.
HATHAWAY. Take it out.
MISS YATES (*taken aback*) Out?
WEMBLEY (*measuring; to George*) Fifteen—twenty-one—thirty-six . . . (*He smiles nastily in Miss Yates' direction*)
HATHAWAY (*silencing Miss Yates with a gesture*) If it's a question of your model or Mr Cosgrove, I don't want any argument.
MISS YATES. But, Mr Hathaway . . .
WEMBLEY (*still listening delightedly*) Forty-one—sixteen and a half . . .
HATHAWAY (*trenchantly*) He happens to be the one reliable buyer I've got.
WEMBLEY. Six and three quarters. (*The smile leaves his face at Hathaway's remark*)

(MISS YATES *fumes*.
HATHAWAY *strides out up* C)

MISS YATES (*furiously*) Well! I must say!

(GEORGE *grins*)

OAKSHOTT (*to Wembley and Miss Yates; cheerily*) Doesn't—(*she crosses to* RC) believe in putting his words through the mincer, does he?

(WALDORF *gets hold of the tape measure and looks curiously at it.*
WEMBLEY *glares at Miss Yates and sees George grinning*)

WEMBLEY (*to George; sharply*) Have you got those?
GEORGE. Yes, Mr Wembley. I got everything.
WEMBLEY (*ignoring the innuendo*) Then come along, please. (*He snatches the measure from Waldorf and moves to the exit up* C)

(MISS YATES *turns to exit up* R)

GEORGE. I'll give you a hand, Miss Yates—in a couple of minutes.
MISS YATES (*coldly*) There's no need, thank you, Miss Jameson is coming.
GEORGE (*eagerly*) Oh—is she all right?

(MISS YATES *exits by the alcove up* R. GEORGE *crosses to follow her off*)

WEMBLEY (*impatiently*) Ingle!
GEORGE (*resignedly*) Coming, Mr Wembley.

(WEMBLEY *exits up* C. GEORGE *hurriedly follows him off.* WALDORF *throughout this, has been standing quite still, a happy smile on his face. He now advances on* OAKSHOTT, *who retreats around the chair* RC, *and circles the table* C, *with* WALDORF *following her. She returns to the chair* RC *and pushes it between them*)

OAKSHOTT. You can sit down, if you want to.
WALDORF. Yes, I found that out. (*He sits on the chair* RC)

(OAKSHOTT *moves* C *and stares at Waldorf*)

WALDORF. At least, I *was* able to. I don't know about now.
OAKSHOTT. You mean you're stiff?
WALDORF. Oh, no—nothing like as stiff as I have been. I used to be stiff all the time.
OAKSHOTT (*eyeing him dryly*) Done this sort of thing before?
WALDORF. No. I haven't.
OAKSHOTT. I hope it'll be a lesson to you.
WALDORF (*happily*) Oh, I'm sure it will. I'm learning something every minute. (*Interestedly*) What's *your* first name?
OAKSHOTT (*sharply*) That'll do.
WALDORF. How pretty!
OAKSHOTT. And don't try anything on with me. I learnt my self-defence in the Force and if you start anything, you won't be the one to finish it.
WALDORF (*puzzled*) Shan't I? Who will, then?
OAKSHOTT (*formidably*) I will. (*She moves* LC)
WALDORF (*with a friendly smile*) I might like that.

(OAKSHOTT *looks very sharply at Waldorf, unable to make him out. The* DOORMAN *enters a little breathlessly up* C)

DOORMAN (*purposefully*) Oakshott! You're wanted in Cosmetics.

Couple of women, this time. Bottles of nail varnish. Caught red-handed.
OAKSHOTT. I can't leave here at the moment.
DOORMAN. You must—one of 'em's violent.

(DAPHNE *enters up* C *and moves to* R *of Waldorf*)

'Sides, it's in your section.
OAKSHOTT (*indicating Waldorf*) He's in my section, too. First come, first served. Look, I can't be in two places at once . . .
DAPHNE (*suddenly*) It's all right—I'll keep an eye on him.

(WALDORF *rises and looks at Daphne.* OAKSHOTT *and the* DOORMAN *look in surprise at Daphne*)

(*Reassuringly*) Miss Yates is just—(*she nods towards the alcove up* R) through there. He'll be all right with the two of us.

(OAKSHOTT *hesitates*)

DOORMAN (*to Oakshott*) He couldn't go far like that, anyhow.
OAKSHOTT. O.K. (*To Daphne*) Well, if he tries anything, give him one below the belt. It'll be self-defence, anyway.

(OAKSHOTT *exits up* C.
The DOORMAN *follows her off.* DAPHNE *immediately turns to* WALDORF, *who sits astride the chair with his arms on the back*)

DAPHNE (*emotionally*) I wanted the chance to speak to you—to apologize—I'm so terribly sorry.

(WALDORF *looks vaguely at Daphne*)

It was the shock—I really thought you were one of the dummies —I didn't give myself time to think, or I never would have given you away. You do believe that, don't you?
WALDORF (*a little dazed by Daphne's vehemence*) Yes, thank you.
DAPHNE (*full of tender sympathy*) Please don't think I haven't any imagination. I have. So much. I know so well how terribly difficult it must be—in some circumstances—to resist temptation. (*Rather suddenly*) Is your wife going to have a baby?
WALDORF. Not today, thank you.
DAPHNE. Oh. She's terribly ill, perhaps? (*She moves down* R) You spent your last shilling on National Health—and then, when you came into the shop—just to get warm for a moment—suddenly everything went black—you had to have something to take back to her—anything . . . (*She moves to* R *of him*) You *are* married?
WALDORF. Not just now, thank you.
DAPHNE (*a little taken aback, but not entirely displeased*) Oh. What made you do it? Was it an impulse? (*She kneels* R *of him*) You saw something you wanted and you just couldn't help yourself? And

Act I MAN ALIVE 31

then—when I was close to you, you couldn't help yourself, either —you had to kiss me, didn't you, even though it meant discovery?
WALDORF. Yes. (*With a gleam in his eye*) Shall I do it again? (*He leans forward*)
DAPHNE (*sitting back on her heels; not angrily*) Certainly not. (*She rises and looks at him with some appreciation*) I've never met anyone quite like you before.
WALDORF. I don't suppose you have.

(GEORGE *enters up* C. *He carries a shirt, socks, shoes, tie and underwear for Waldorf.* DAPHNE *is not altogether pleased at this interruption. She turns to the dressing-table and adjusts the items on it*)

GEORGE (*moving down* C) Hullo, Daphne—are you O.K.?
DAPHNE. Yes—quite, thank you.
GEORGE (*in surprise*) Where's Oakshott? (*He puts the clothing on the bed*)
DAPHNE. Oakshott had to go for a minute.
GEORGE (*with a glance at Waldorf; horrified*) Doesn't she know what he did? He might have done the same thing again.
DAPHNE (*rather shortly*) Of course not.
GEORGE. Anything might have happened.

(WEMBLEY *bustles in up* C. *He carries a suit, a hat and an overcoat, which he puts on the bed*)

WEMBLEY (*to Waldorf*) Now then you'll get into these——

(WALDORF *rises*)

—and kindly remember they're not your property. Keep your hands out of the pockets, don't spill anything and don't sit down more than you have to. (*He crosses to Waldorf*) Let me have the gown, please. (*He helps Waldorf to take off the dressing-gown*)

(DAPHNE *watches unhappily.*
MISS YATES *enters by the alcove up* R. WALDORF *moves towards Daphne as the gown is pulled off. His right arm sticks in the sleeve and he is pulled to* WEMBLEY, *who tugs the sleeve free*)

MISS YATES (*impatiently*) Miss Jameson.
DAPHNE. Oh—I was just coming, Miss Yates. (*She moves towards the alcove up* R)
WEMBLEY (*giving the dressing-gown to George*) This can go back on display. (*To Waldorf*) Now, the pyjamas.
MISS YATES. Not in here. Miss Jameson and I are just coming in.
WEMBLEY (*irritated*) You heard what Mr Hathaway said—he can't go through Corsets.
MISS YATES (*indicating the alcove up* L; *impatiently*) Well, take him in the back there. (*She nods to Daphne to follow her*)

(Miss Yates *exits by the alcove up* R.
Daphne *follows her off*)

Wembley (*looking after Miss Yates; fuming*) Really—that woman! (*He pushes Waldorf towards the alcove up* L) There are moments when it's extremely hard to remember the team spirit.

(Hathaway *enters up* C)

Hathaway (*briskly*) Now then—I want this window back into action (*His brow darkens as he sees Waldorf. Exasperated*) Still here?
Wembley (*hastily*) We're just getting him dressed, Mr Hathaway. At least, now, he'll be a credit in court to our Men's Tailoring. (*He motions Waldorf towards the alcove up* L) In there. (*To Waldorf. Severely*) And then you're going straight to Marlborough Street Police Station.
Waldorf (*with genuine interest*) Shall I enjoy that?
Wembley. If you enjoy seven days without the option.

(Wembley *bustles* Waldorf *into the alcove up* L, *follows him off, and draws the curtains*. George, *with the dressing-gown, moves down* L *and looks around the window, rather perplexed*)

George (*bewildered*) That's a funny thing . . .
Hathaway. What is?
George. I just discovered something, sir. It's not only his clothes that are missing. The model's gone, too.
Hathaway. Model?
George (*indicating the dressing-gown*) That this was on. The one he took the place of. There's no sign of it—anywhere.

(Miss Yates *and* Daphne *propel the chaise in through the alcove up* R, *feet first*. Belgravia *is still lying on it, in the housecoat, but now, instead of the book, she is holding in her hands a large aluminium saucepan and a whisk*. Miss Yates *and* Daphne *set the chaise* C)

Belgravia. Well, that was a surrealist five minutes to say the least.

(Miss Yates *takes the whisk out of Belgravia's hand and stands* R *of the chaise*. Daphne *stands above the chaise*)

George (*to Hathaway*) It's disappeared completely. There's something funny been going on here.

(Miss Yates *and* Daphne *look curiously at George*)

Hathaway. Nonsense! Even if he smashed the model, the pieces must be somewhere. Dammit, he can't have . . .
Wembley (*off*) Aaaaah!

(Wembley *enters through the curtains from the alcove up* L. *His expression is distraught and he is a little unsteady on his feet. He crosses*

ACT I   MAN ALIVE   33

to the chaise, pushes Belgravia's feet to the floor and sits on the chaise. This moves BELGRAVIA's head next to his)

(*Hoarsely*) Mr Hathaway . . . Ingle . . . Pheno-Barbitone!
HATHAWAY. Wembley! What is it?
WEMBLEY. The name—it's just what he said it was! (*He sways*) He must be what he said he was, too!
HATHAWAY. Wembley, explain yourself.
WEMBLEY. It's stamped on his—lower back, sir. It was horrible. (*He looks* R, *comes face to face with Belgravia and pushes her back so that her feet go in the air. He pushes her feet down*)
HATHAWAY. Stamped on his what? What the blazes are you talking about?
WEMBLEY. I saw it with my own eyes, Mr Hathaway. It says: "Number eight-seven-six-four-eight-two. Made in England. The Waldorf—(*he swallows*) Patent Pending".

(WALDORF, *in his pyjamas, enters by the alcove up* L *and crosses to* LC. *The others stare at Wembley in astonishment, and then stare at Waldorf, with dawning realization*)

WALDORF (*to Wembley; happily*) Shall I show them, too? (*He starts to undo the cord of his pyjamas trousers*)
WEMBLEY (*frantically*) No, don't let him!

The CURTAIN *quickly falls*

ACT II

Scene—*The same. Half an hour later.*
The curtains of the alcove up L *are open. The lighting is for "blind down" and the window is in a state of flux. The chaise has been removed. On the telephone table up* LC *there are some price cards, a box of pins, a tape measure, an ink pad and a rubber stamp.*

When the Curtain *rises,* Belgravia *and* Jubilee, *covered with brown paper sheets, are standing* RC, *Jubilee* L *of Belgravia.*

Jubilee (*in an interested tone*) I hear they got to the bottom of it.
Belgravia. What a gift you have for the *mot-juste*.
Jubilee. Of course, I only know the barest details . . .
Belgravia. Jubilee! *Please*.
Jubilee. I only wish I'd been here. I always seem to miss the most exciting moments. Like that smash-and-grab you were in last October.
Belgravia. You'd have been welcome to that. I was very nearly hit by the brick.
Jubilee. They took a mink coat off you, didn't they?
Belgravia. They did. I had nothing on at all underneath. That made the fur department look pretty ridiculous.
Jubilee. What happened this morning—*exactly?*
Belgravia. You mean *after* the barest details? Everything. Wembley went even more Wembley than usual, George goggled, that Yates woman just raised her eyebrows and Mr Hathaway, as always at moments of crisis, ordered the entire window taken out and re-dressed.
Jubilee. So that's why we're back, after all.
Belgravia. Yes. He then sent up to Sister and they all had sedatives—on the house.
Jubilee (*enjoying the account*) It must have been even worse than stocktaking. Poor Mr Hathaway.
Belgravia. Poor Waldorf, if you ask me. Projected into that world of theirs without a by-your-leave or a beg-your-pardon. I think *he's* the one that should have had the sedative.
Jubilee. Where is he now?
Belgravia. He's gone with Oakshott, to get his National Insurance card.
Jubilee. Insurance? Oh, well, I suppose shop fittings don't really cover him any longer.
Belgravia (*sadly*) No. Like it or not, poor Waldorf comes in the human being class now. He can have his fill of influenza, the Inland Revenue, the Iron Curtain and the washing-up.

ACT II   MAN ALIVE

JUBILEE (*shrewdly*) You quite took a fancy to him, didn't you?
BELGRAVIA (*a little too emphatically*) Nonsense! I can sympathize, can't I, without you jumping to a lot of ridiculous sentimental conclusions?
JUBILEE. Certainly, dear. I admit, of course, he wasn't much to look at . . .
BELGRAVIA. You know perfectly well he was extremely handsome. Stock size, real artificial hair and until this awful thing happened to him, one of the most beautiful fixed expressions I've ever seen.
JUBILEE. Hey-ho!
BELGRAVIA. I don't know why we have to speak as though he were dead, just because he's come to life.
JUBILEE. Well, from our point of view, it's much the same thing, isn't it?
BELGRAVIA. I suppose it is.

(MISS YATES *enters up* C. *She carries three show cards. She moves* L, *selects one card, places the others on the chair, then crosses and stands between Jubilee and Belgravia*)

In any case, the only effect he's had on me is to give me one of the most disrupting mornings I've ever had—not even counting last Easter, when that little ass Daphne mislaid my head for half an hour.
JUBILEE. Well, there's no need to get in such a wax about it.
BELGRAVIA. That expression, even when used by human beings, has always struck me as completely meaningless. For people of our composition, it seems to me in addition to be in extremely poor taste.

(MISS YATES *unpins the paper on Belgravia's right shoulder, and on Jubilee's left shoulder*)

JUBILEE. Oh, dear, you are in a huff this morning, aren't you?
BELGRAVIA. Am I? I suppose I am.

(MISS YATES, *standing between Belgravia and Jubilee, pulls off the brown paper, revealing them to be dressed in long white woollen combinations*)

(*Bitterly*) I am also in what quite obviously must have been an unsaleable line for the past forty years.

(MISS YATES *pins a show card to Belgravia's bosom*)

What does that say?
JUBILEE. "Unrepeatable."

(MISS YATES *raises Belgravia's arms and puts her hands behind her head*)

BELGRAVIA. It sums up my feelings on the subject with a very high degree of accuracy.

(DAPHNE *enters up* C. *She carries a large pink powder-puff, a loofah, a scent spray and an inflated rubber bathing ring with a fish's head*)

DAPHNE (*a little breathless*) I'm sorry, Miss Yates . . . (*She puts all but the ring on the chair* L)

MISS YATES. It shouldn't have taken you five minutes to collect those. (*She puts Belgravia's arms akimbo*)

DAPHNE (*crossing and putting the ring on Jubilee's left arm*) The girls kept stopping me and asking questions. I tried telling the truth, but of course, they didn't believe that. (*She picks up the brown paper*) The whole place is buzzing with rumours. One of the juniors in Baby Linen, said she heard I'd been coshed by a maniac and then lost my honour in here, with the blind up and a card saying "Fifteen and elevenpence. For Personal Shoppers Only". (*She throws the paper behind the alcove curtains up* R *then moves to* R *of Belgravia*) I just said we didn't have anything at that price.

(MISS YATES *concentrates on Belgravia, trying different poses and stepping back to judge the effect*)

MISS YATES (*abstractedly*) I expect she was thinking of the catalogue. Just try it sideways.

(DAPHNE *turns* BELGRAVIA *so that she faces* L)

No. Back to the front.

(DAPHNE *turns* BELGRAVIA *to face front, then crosses to* L *of Jubilee*)

(*Thoughtfully*) It seems to lack something.

BELGRAVIA. If you ask me it ought to lack a great deal more.

MISS YATES (*pointing to the chair* L) Let me have one or two of those.

(DAPHNE *crosses and picks up the loofah and puff, then stares abstractedly ahead of her*)

JUBILEE. Oh, for a nice liberty bodice.
BELGRAVIA. Oh, for just liberty.
MISS YATES (*sharply*) Miss Jameson! (*She holds out her hand for the accessories*)

DAPHNE (*handing the loofah and puff to Miss Yates*) I'm sorry, Miss Yates. (*She crosses and picks up the spray*)

(MISS YATES *tries the puff in Belgravia's left hand*)

I don't know how you can go on working—with all this excitement.

MISS YATES (*rejecting the powder-puff*) In the middle of a Sale,

I've really got no time to worry about the supernatural. (*She tries the loofah in Belgravia's right hand and pushes her arm straight up*)
DAPHNE. Well, he may be supernatural, but he's terribly good looking, isn't he?
MISS YATES. Naturally. The manufacturers did the best they could. (*She takes the loofah out of Belgravia's hand and puts the puff in its place*)
BELGRAVIA. I don't know what I've done to deserve this.

(MISS YATES *moves Belgravia's arm so that the puff gags her*)
JUBILEE. Oh, come, come. You've modelled underwear often enough. You were months and months in brassieres.

(MISS YATES *moves Belgravia's arm down again*)
BELGRAVIA (*bitterly*) Yes. That was very uplifting.

(MISS YATES *puts the loofah in Belgravia's left hand, but is still dissatisfied*)
MISS YATES. No. No, I'm afraid not. (*She removes the puff and loofah*) Now. What else have we?
BELGRAVIA. Why not give me an umbrella and be done with it?

(MISS YATES *hands the loofah and puff to Daphne, takes the spray and squirts it once or twice to test it.*
GEORGE *enters up* C. *He carries a blazer, a pair of grey flannels and some cardigans*)

MISS YATES (*to George*) Where's Mr Wembley? (*Sarcastically*) Doesn't he want his half of the window?
GEORGE. He won't be long. He had to run up a few minutes ago and lie down, with Sister.
MISS YATES. What, again?
GEORGE (*moving to the alcove up* L) The sedative went to his head a bit. (*He puts the clothing in the alcove*)

(MISS YATES *puts the spray in Jubilee's right hand, and the bulb in her left.* DAPHNE *crosses to the chair* L.
HATHAWAY *enters purposefully up* C. *He looks worried*)

HATHAWAY (*moving down* C; *to Miss Yates*) Oakshott not back with him yet? (*He stares in horror at Belgravia and Jubilee*) What in the name of heaven . . . ? (*Irritably*) Miss Yates, we're supposed to be a twentieth century store . . .

(GEORGE *moves down* L)

MISS YATES. Well, I thought it was strange, Mr Hathaway, but you did say . . .
HATHAWAY (*crossing and standing down* R; *exasperated*) I said some kind of attractive combination. For the two of them. I

meant a day dress and an afternoon. Or an evening and a party frock. Anything. Certainly anything but these. (*He moves to* R *of Jubilee*) Look at this fiddling thing. (*He squeezes the bulb of the spray and gets sprayed*)

MISS YATES. I'm sorry, Mr Hathaway—in all the confusion I didn't like to query—I'll change them. (*She moves towards Jubilee*)

HATHAWAY (*impatiently*) Not now—I've something of importance to say. (*He moves down* C)

(WEMBLEY *enters up* C.

FRED *follows him on and stands up* L. WEMBLEY, *looking a little sickly, moves down* RC)

(*Forcefully*) Wembley!

WEMBLEY (*quivering a little*) Yes, Mr Hathaway?

HATHAWAY. Pay attention, please. And everyone. (*He crosses and stands down* R) Despite my hopes to the contrary, the commotion in this window has already given rise to rumours. If the facts were to leak out—it might very well endanger the entire success of this year's January Sale.

GEORGE (*moving* LC) Excuse me, sir—but couldn't it be sort of good publicity?

(WEMBLEY *frowns at George for interrupting*)

HATHAWAY (*forcefully*) It most emphatically could *not*. It's a proven fact that any distraction from the merchandise can only be harmful in the extreme. We had a window full of cuckoo clocks some years ago. Customers spent so much of their time watching for the first cuckoo that they had none left in which to do any shopping.

JUBILEE. I was in the next window. At the end of the week I was going cuckoo myself.

HATHAWAY (*moving between Belgravia and Jubilee*) I'm taking no such risk this time. (*He looks at the price tag on the spray*) Excellent value. You will please note, as from now, that the—er—(*he moves to* L *of Jubilee*) phenomenon with which we were confronted this morning, did not, in fact, take place. Is that quite clear? (*He looks at the price tag on the ring*) Very reasonable. (*He looks behind Wembley's lapel*) No price tag? Oh! Oh! It's you. (*He moves down* RC) In that case, the sooner this window is back in service and the whole incident forgotten, the better.

DAPHNE (*looking at Hathaway*) But—what about *him*, Mr Hathaway?

HATHAWAY. Who?

DAPHNE. The—Waldorf.

HATHAWAY. That is my concern. (*In a tone of dismissal*) In any case, you can rest assured you won't be bothered any further. (*He crosses and stands down* L)

MISS YATES (*to Daphne*) And don't bother Mr Hathaway. (*She

ACT II MAN ALIVE 39

indicates Belgravia's combinations) Help me off with these. (*She starts to unbutton Belgravia's combinations*)

(DAPHNE *crosses reluctantly to Miss Yates*)

HATHAWAY. Not in here, please, Miss Yates. I'm trying to think.

MISS YATES (*indicating the alcove up* R; *to Daphne*) In there. (*She calls*) Fred—Mr Ingle.

(MISS YATES *and* DAPHNE *exit by the alcove up* R. FRED *and* GEORGE *cross to Belgravia and Jubilee*)

JUBILEE. Oh, surely they're not going to put us in Ironmongery.

(GEORGE *picks* JUBILEE *up and carries her off by the alcove up* R. FRED *bends Belgravia forward and hoists her over his shoulder*)

BELGRAVIA. No, Gramophones, I expect. (*She sings*) "I'm dreaming of a white Christmas. . . ."

(FRED *carries* BELGRAVIA *off by the alcove up* R. HATHAWAY *paces thoughtfully to* R)

WEMBLEY. Might I make a suggestion, Mr Hathaway?
HATHAWAY (*stopping and turning*) Well?

(GEORGE *enters by the alcove up* R, *crosses and stands down* L)

WEMBLEY. I think we should send him back to the makers, with a complaint.

HATHAWAY (*exasperated*) The problem, Wembley, is to suppress all news of this. Certainly not to play straight into the hands of some publicity-seeking firm of suppliers, whoever they are. Who are they?

(WEMBLEY *wordlessly shakes his head*)

GEORGE. Shopcraft Limited, sir—I checked the invoice. But, if you don't mind my saying so, sir—I don't think it was so much the model as the lamp.

HATHAWAY (*puzzled*) The lamp?
GEORGE (*nodding towards the sun-lamp*) The U.V. I think that's what did it. After all, sir, what first created life upon this earth, sir?

WEMBLEY. Really, Ingle—this is no time to bother Mr Hathaway about the Creation.

HATHAWAY. Wembley, please. (*To George*) Well?
GEORGE. Well, it was the sun, sir, wasn't it? And what is the sun, very largely, but a concentrated source of ultra-violet rays? This is a new model, sir. Extra strong radiation. Well—supposing the radiation was just a bit too strong—the violet was a bit too ultra, so to speak . . .

HATHAWAY (*impressed*) You may very well be right. (*To Wembley*) Who supplied this thing?
WEMBLEY. Well, I don't quite . . .
GEORGE. Olux Lamps, sir—Park Royal. I checked their invoice at the same time.
HATHAWAY (*crossing to George*) You're an intelligent boy. Remind me about it.
GEORGE (*happily*) Thank you very much, sir.
HATHAWAY (*looking despairingly at the lamp*) How many dozen of those have we got?
GEORGE. Only the one, sir, as a matter of fact. It's the demonstration model. The rest are due today.
HATHAWAY. Yes—well, I shall get on to these people and tell them they can keep the lot. *And* have this one back. We've had quite enough of a demonstration already. (*To Wembley*) You'd better go straight to Despatch, tell them to collect this and send it back immediately.
WEMBLEY (*moving hastily to the exit up* C) Yes, Mr Hathaway.
HATHAWAY. It's to go today. Priority.
WEMBLEY (*without stopping*) Yes, Mr Hathaway.

(WEMBLEY *exits up* C. HATHAWAY *moves towards the exit up* C.
DAPHNE *enters by the alcove up* R, *plucks up her courage, and steps forward to speak to Hathaway*)

DAPHNE. Oh—Mr Hathaway——

(HATHAWAY *pauses, exasperated*)

—I've been thinking—and if it would be any help for tonight—I'll take Waldorf home with me.

(HATHAWAY *stares at Daphne, his anger rising*)

GEORGE (*horror-struck*) What!
DAPHNE (*blithely unaware of Hathaway's anger*) We've got a nice spare room and I'm sure mother wouldn't mind . . .

(MISS YATES *enters by the alcove up* R)

MISS YATES (*exasperatedly*) Miss Jameson, I *asked* you to go to the stock-room.
HATHAWAY (*boiling over*) Miss Jameson—I have not the slightest intention of allowing this Waldorf thing to go wandering at large, stating his name and displaying his identification particulars to every Tom, Dick and Harry in Greater London. Not even your mother.

(*There is a moment's silence.*
OAKSHOTT *enters up* C. *There is something of a change in her manner, more of the woman and less of the police*)

OAKSHOTT (*cheerfully*) Not in here, I suppose?

(*The others stare at Oakshott*)

(*She moves to* R *of Hathaway*) Waldorf, I mean? (*She moves down* C)

(MISS YATES *and* DAPHNE *move down* RC)

HATHAWAY (*moving down* LC; *sensing disaster*) Isn't he with you?
OAKSHOTT. Mislaid him in the Fancy Goods, sir, about ten minutes ago. You know what the crowds are, Sale time. He was rather sweet, he insisted on my going first . . .
HATHAWAY. Oh, Great Missenden!

(*They all move up stage*)

OAKSHOTT (*reassuringly*) He'll be quite O.K., Mr Hathaway. He's in the store, *somewhere*.
HATHAWAY (*infuriated*) Somewhere!

(*They all move down stage*)

Anywhere may be fatal. He's got to be found. (*He moves to the exit up* C)
OAKSHOTT (*moving to the exit up* C) Leave it to me, sir.
HATHAWAY. Not this time. (*To George*) Don't stand there. Come along. Come along!
GEORGE (*with a glance at Daphne*) Don't worry, sir. I'll get hold of him.

(HATHAWAY *and* OAKSHOTT *exit hurriedly up* C. GEORGE *crosses to the exit up* C)

DAPHNE (*agitatedly*) George! No!

(GEORGE *dashes out up* C. DAPHNE *starts to hurry after him*)

MISS YATES (*scandalized*) Miss Jameson!

(DAPHNE, *heedless, runs out up* C *after George*.

MISS YATES *stands a moment, fuming, then with an infuriated shrug, exits by the alcove up* L. *There is a brief pause.*

WALDORF *enters up* C. *He is smartly dressed in a painfully new suit, overcoat, hat and shoes, and carries a carrier bag with "Hathaway's" on the outside. His manner is happy and unruffled. He hangs the carrier on the back of the chair* R *of the exit up* C, *then looks into the alcove up* R)

WALDORF (*calling*) Annabelle! (*Seeing the window apparently deserted he shrugs lightheartedly and turns to go*)

(MISS YATES *enters by the alcove up* L)

MISS YATES (*hastily*) Oh! Just a moment.

(WALDORF *turns. His face lights up*)

WALDORF. Oh. Hullo, Miss Yates. (*He raises his hat*) I'm glad to see you.

MISS YATES (*advancing a little*) I'm—very glad to see *you*.

WALDORF. I lost the Oakshott I was with, somewhere. So many people—women a great many of them—I'm afraid I didn't look where I was going—I suppose I ought to try and find her. (*He turns to go*)

MISS YATES. Oh—no. I wouldn't do that.

WALDORF (*stopping and turning*) You wouldn't?

MISS YATES. No. Stay here—and probably she'll come and find you.

(WALDORF *nods*)

Why don't you take your things off?

WALDORF. All of them?

MISS YATES. Your overcoat, I mean.

WALDORF. Oh. (*He suddenly gives her a dazzling smile*) Well, if you'd like me to, I will. (*He removes his hat and puts it on the chair with the carrier bag. He is unaccustomed to the buttons of his overcoat and tries to unscrew them*)

MISS YATES (*moving to Waldorf*) Let me help you off with it. (*She manipulates the buttons with a professional flick of the wrist*)

WALDORF (*delighted*) Thank you. (*He smiles charmingly and removes his overcoat*)

(MISS YATES *picks up the hat and puts it with the overcoat on the bed*)

(*He unbuttons his jacket, with a similar flick of the wrist. Politely*) Can I help *you* off with anything?

MISS YATES (*a shade taken aback*) Not just now, thank you. She gestures to the chair R of the exit up C and the chair L) Shall we? (*She moves the chair L to LC*)

WALDORF. Thank you. (*He moves the chair R of the exit and places it very close to the chair LC*)

(MISS YATES *moves the chair L a little distance away and sits*. WALDORF *moves his chair nearer to Miss Yates and sits. Throughout the scene that follows, he keeps looking admiringly at* MISS YATES, *who gradually begins to succumb in spite of herself*)

I've got my National Insurance card. Would you like to see it?

MISS YATES (*politely*) Thank you very much.

WALDORF (*taking the card from his pocket*) They wanted evidence of my identity there, too, but the Oakshott wouldn't let me show the girl behind the counter. She said she could take it as read.

Nice girl. She had green eyes. (*He indicates the card which he hands to Miss Yates*) Much the same colour as that.

(MISS YATES *looks at the card*)

You see—I've got two names now—and a number. That shows I'm a genuine British citizen.

MISS YATES (*reading*) "Waldorf Patent-Pending."

WALDORF (*leaning close and pointing*) That's a hyphen.

MISS YATES (*leaning away from him*) I noticed it. Looks quite aristocratic. (*She returns the card to Waldorf*)

WALDORF (*with a charming smile*) Have *you* another name, Miss Yates?

MISS YATES (*rising and drawing her chair a little* L) I have, but I leave it at home when I come to work in the morning.

WALDORF. In that case, I suppose, no-one here can use it? (*He slides on to Miss Yates' chair*)

MISS YATES. No. (*She crosses above Waldorf to* R *of his chair*)

WALDORF. And who uses it there? (*He slides back on to his own chair*)

MISS YATES. Well—no-one, actually. (*She moves down* C) I live by myself.

WALDORF (*rising and moving to* L *of her*) That seems rather a waste, doesn't it?

MISS YATES. It never occurred to me that way.

WALDORF. Perhaps I could go home with you in the evening and use it?

MISS YATES. No. I hardly think that.

WALDORF. Why not?

MISS YATES. Well—when you've been a fully grown man rather longer, you'll know all about it.

WALDORF. You've been a fully grown woman some time, I suppose?

MISS YATES (*a little nettled*) I'm forty-one.

WALDORF (*interested*) Bust or hips?

MISS YATES (*angrily*) Years.

WALDORF. I see. Then—you're not what they call a Junior Miss?

MISS YATES. No—I'm a rather Senior Miss. (*She smiles*)

WALDORF. That's the first time I've seen you smile. Perhaps you generally leave that at home, too, every morning?

MISS YATES (*moving* RC) I think I very likely do.

WALDORF. What *do* you bring, then?

MISS YATES. A certain amount of efficiency. Mr Wembley may have other views, but *I* think I'm a first-class buyer.

WALDORF (*vaguely*) I seem to remember someone saying something of the kind.

MISS YATES (*pleased*) They did?

WALDORF. I think so. A first-class something, anyway. (*He is*

about to move towards her again, when he catches sight of the carrier bag on the chair) Oh. (*With a charming smile*) I have something in here for you. (*He moves to the carrier bag and opens it*)
MISS YATES (*surprised*) Me?
WALDORF. I saw it and I thought it would—(*he takes an attractive silk scarf from the bag*) bring out the colour of your eyes. (*He smiles hopefully at her*)
MISS YATES (*touched*) How very—thoughtful of you.
WALDORF (*moving to Miss Yates*) May I? (*He holds out the scarf to put it around her neck*)
MISS YATES (*staring at the scarf*) But—you haven't any money. How did you get it?
WALDORF. It wasn't any trouble. There were plenty of them. (*He puts the scarf around her neck and admires the result*) It does. Very well. Very well indeed.

(MISS YATES *turns involuntarily to look in the dressing-table mirror*)

Don't you think so?

(MISS YATES *for a moment is completely feminine, as she looks in the mirror, then she recovers herself and turns away*)

MISS YATES. It probably does—but none the less . . . (*She removes the scarf and moves toward the exit up* C)
WALDORF (*restraining her*) D'you know what I think? I think that just for once, you ought to try the opposite.
MISS YATES (*his hands still touching hers*) The opposite?
WALDORF. Leave at home what you usually bring and bring what you generally leave at home.

(MISS YATES *smiles*)

That's what I mean. (*He moves close to her*) Don't you think so—(*he puts the scarf around her neck*) thingummy jig?
MISS YATES (*a little indignantly*) Rose.
WALDORF (*softly*) Rose. (*He pulls her to him with the scarf and kisses her*)

(MISS YATES *responds. As they come out of the embrace she is a little breathless, and astonished at herself*)

MISS YATES. I've never done a thing like that before in my life.
WALDORF (*happily*) Invigorating, isn't it?

(OAKSHOTT *enters briskly up* C *and moves down* LC)

OAKSHOTT (*relieved*) Oh—you found him?

Miss Yates (*none too comfortable*) Yes. (*With an apparently casual movement she removes the scarf from Oakshott's eyeline*)

(Oakshott, *in any case, is looking at Waldorf*)

(*To Oakshott*) Excuse me—I—have to go and settle up about something.

(Miss Yates, *looking romantically at Waldorf, moves to the entrance up* C, *turns to go, bumps into the wall, and exits up* C, *rather hurriedly*)

Waldorf (*advancing on Oakshott; with a happy look on his face*) Hullo, Annabelle.

Oakshott. Hullo, Wal. (*Girlishly reproachful*) You naughty old thing—(*she moves to* L *of Waldorf*) What happened to you?

Waldorf. I looked for you everywhere. I even went back to the soda fountain.

Oakshott (*a little anxiously*) You didn't tell her—(*she nods towards the exit up* C) we had a rum sundae?

Waldorf. No. Should I have?

Oakshott. You mustn't tell anyone. Mr Hathaway wouldn't like it.

Waldorf. *I* liked it. That was the first food I ever tasted.

Oakshott (*smiling at him*) Well, you have to start somewhere, don't you?

Waldorf (*nodding; seriously*) Not only with food. (*Politely*) Why don't you take your things off?

(Oakshott *shoots Waldorf a shrewd glance, then crosses to the dressing-table*)

Oakshott. I'm quite all right as I am, thank you. Phew! I've been through about ten departments in three minutes. (*She puts her handbag on the stool and looks at herself in the mirror*)

Waldorf. She said she hadn't seen you.

Oakshott. Who said?

Waldorf. The girl at the soda fountain. Oh, it was wonderful. (*Dreamily*) I never knew anything could look so cool and make you feel so warm. (*He moves to the bed*)

Oakshott (*turning; smiling*) Rum sundaes are like that.

Waldorf (*sitting on the bed*) Not only rum sundaes. (*Politely*) Shall we? (*He gestures and lies back*)

Oakshott (*severely*) Wal!

(Waldorf *sits up*)

I'm not altogether sure I should have given you one at all.

Waldorf (*rising*) Why not?

Oakshott. Never you mind.

Waldorf (*crossing to her*) D'you think when I've been a fully grown man rather longer I shall know all about it?

Oakshott (*moving to the chairs* LC) I think you know quite

enough to be going on with. Starting that sort of thing before you're even a week old.

WALDORF (*crossing to her*) You said if I started anything you might be the one to finish it.

OAKSHOTT. That was purely professional. (*She stands between the chairs*) I thought you'd been up to something in my department.

WALDORF (*sitting on the chair* R *of Oakshott*) What department is that?

OAKSHOTT. People who help themselves to what they want, when nobody's looking. Like—(*she glances towards the exit up* C *then suddenly kisses him; breathlessly*) that. (*She moves the chair* L *of her close to Waldorf, and sits*)

(WALDORF *smiles happily*)

You know, Wal—it's funny, but I think you've got something for me.

WALDORF (*as he suddenly remembers; brightly*) I have. (*Instead of kissing her in return, as she expects, he suddenly rises and looks into the carrier bag*) I saw it and I thought it would—(*he looks up and smiles*) bring out the colour of your eyes.

OAKSHOTT (*melting*) Oh, Wal.

(WALDORF *takes a scarf from the carrier, identical with the one he gave to Miss Yates*)

(*She stares aghast at the scarf*) Wal! That's not wrapped! (*She rises*)

WALDORF (*lifting the scarf towards her neck*) May I?

OAKSHOTT (*agitatedly*) Look, you'd better give that to me. (*She takes the scarf from him*)

WALDORF (*happily*) That's what I brought it for.

(DAPHNE, *concern on her face, enters up* C *and then, relieved, moves down* RC)

DAPHNE. Oh—thank goodness. He's with you.

OAKSHOTT. Yes. (*She puts the scarf behind her back*) Thank goodness he is.

DAPHNE. Miss Yates said he'd been found. Oh, by the way, they're asking for you at the scarf counter.

OAKSHOTT (*moving hastily towards the exit up* C) Yes, I had an idea they might be.

(OAKSHOTT *exits up* C)

WALDORF (*directing his smile at Daphne*) Hullo, Miss Jameson.

DAPHNE (*crossing to* R *of Waldorf; solicitously*) Are you all right? If anyone's put a finger on you . . . Have they?

WALDORF (*rather sadly*) Nothing to speak of. (*Brightening*) But you have to start somewhere, don't you?

DAPHNE (*warmly*) No-one's going to touch a hair of your head.
WALDORF (*disappointed*) Never?

(DAPHNE *shakes her head*)

Oh!
DAPHNE (*moving* R; *emotionally*) The world must seem so huge and so friendless. But you have got a friend. (*She moves to Waldorf*)

(WALDORF *starts to speak*)

No, don't try to stop me. I don't care what the consequences are—if they won't let me take you home—(*she moves close to him*) then I shall stay behind when the store closes and spend the night here with you——

(WALDORF *puts his hands on her arms*)

—(*she backs a pace*) in different departments, of course. Oh, Waldorf . . . (*Apropros the name*) You don't mind, do you?
WALDORF (*happily*) I don't mind anything.
DAPHNE. You'll never be just another cuckoo-clock to me.

(WALDORF *gazes a little pensively at her*)

To me, you're something wonderful—a new life that . . . What are you staring at?
WALDORF. The colour of your eyes. I wasn't sure for a moment —(*brightening*) but I think it'll really bring it out rather well. (*He turns to the carrier bag*)

(DAPHNE *looks bewildered*. WALDORF *produces a similar scarf to the others*)

DAPHNE (*touched*) Oh—Waldorf.

(WALDORF *takes a bunch of roses from the carrier*)

WALDORF. Oh! And I picked these for you, too.
DAPHNE. Picked them? But—where?
WALDORF. In the Flower Department. (*He moves to her*) May I? (*He puts the scarf around her neck, then hands her the roses*)
DAPHNE. That's terribly sweet of you. (*She removes the scarf, and looks at the roses, both touched and rather worried at the same time*) I'll—just have to go and—put these in water. (*She gestures with the scarf, then hastily indicates the flowers and smiles reassuringly at him*) You stay here. (*She turns to go, then pauses*) No, you'd better go in there. (*She leads him towards the alcove up* R) You'll be safer.
WALDORF (*anxiously*) They both will—won't they?

(DAPHNE *looks puzzled*)

Bring out the . . . (*He gestures at her eyes*)
DAPHNE. Beautifully. I love flowers—roses, especially. I don't suppose you knew they *were* roses, did you?

WALDORF. No. (*With a charming smile*) I thought they were Mr Hathaway's.

(DAPHNE *smiles*.

WALDORF *exits by the alcove up* R. DAPHNE *looks after him for a moment, and then at the flowers. She moves to the dressing-table, puts the scarf on her head and, holding the roses, gazes at herself in the mirror.*

GEORGE *enters up* C *and moves down* RC)

GEORGE (*purposefully*) Daphne . . .

DAPHNE (*rather shortly*) It's all right. (*She whips the scarf from her head*) He's been found.

GEORGE (*standing his ground*) I know that.

DAPHNE (*crossing to* LC) Then you don't need to worry any more.

GEORGE (*a little belligerently*) Don't I? (*He moves down* C. *Forcefully*) What's all this about tonight, I'd like to know?

DAPHNE (*anxious lest Waldorf should hear*) Ssh! They'll hear you inside. (*She glances towards the exit up* C)

GEORGE (*with some heat*) I don't care. You must have taken leave of your senses.

DAPHNE (*on her dignity*) I can't stop now and I refuse to discuss it. (*She moves to the exit up* C)

GEORGE (*following Daphne; fuming*) Offer to go taking home a thing like that.

DAPHNE (*stopping and turning; in an indignant undertone*) He's *not* a thing!

GEORGE. I'd like to know what else. Delivered on Saturday by Shopcraft Limited.

DAPHNE (*moving down* L) I don't care what he was on Saturday. He isn't the same now.

GEORGE. Nor are you, it seems. (*Bitterly*) And just when we can probably get married. The old man told me to remind him, and you know that means a raise.

DAPHNE. I can't help it. (*Emotionally*) He's like a little lost child, and if no-one else is going to protect and take care of him, *I shall.*

GEORGE (*moving down* C) Whether he asks you to or not, I suppose?

DAPHNE. He doesn't have to ask. (*Romantically*) In a way, I feel that I brought him into the world.

GEORGE. *What!*

DAPHNE. You seem to forget—I was with him—here—in the window . . .

GEORGE. Yes. And I seem to remember, he didn't behave much like a little lost child at the time.

DAPHNE. Poor lamb! He didn't even realize what he was doing. (*She smells the flowers*)

GEORGE (*forcefully*) And *you* don't *now*. (*He indicates the flowers*) What are those?
DAPHNE. Something he took the trouble to give me.
GEORGE (*bitterly*) For Mother's Day, I suppose?
DAPHNE (*ignoring this*) Just because they bring out the colour of my eyes. (*Dreamily*) There's something so fresh and unspoiled about him . . .
GEORGE. Fresh is right. If you ask me he's a menace.
DAPHNE. I don't ask you. Except just to leave him alone, that's all.
GEORGE. I wouldn't touch him with a barge pole. And if you've got a grain of sense, you'll stop messing about with something you don't understand. (*He moves* RC) A thing like him might do anything.
DAPHNE (*crossing to him; angrily*) If you call him a thing once more . . .
GEORGE. Well, he is a thing. Brought him into the world! What brought him into the world was just a bunch of rays at one end of the spectrum.
DAPHNE (*angry and decisive*) All right, George—that's the finish. (*She moves* L)
GEORGE. If it had been the other end, for all we know . . . (*He breaks off as he has a sudden thought*) The other end. Daphne!
DAPHNE (*icily*) And as for getting married, I'm just glad I found out in time. (*She moves up* C)·
GEORGE (*taken aback*) What! (*He moves to* R *of her*)
DAPHNE. Otherwise it would only have meant a divorce. (*She turns to go*)
GEORGE (*agitatedly*) Listen—Daphne—just because that . . . Hang it! *I've* given you flowers dozens of times.
DAPHNE (*turning; with supreme contempt*) Yes. Just what you've paid for.

(DAPHNE *exits up* C. GEORGE *starts to follow her*)

GEORGE (*utterly dumbfounded*) What! Listen, Daphne, I think I can . . . (*He realizes she has gone, turns, crosses to the sun-lamp, looks at it with mounting determination and moves it a little*)

(WEMBLEY, *looking agitated, enters up* C)

WEMBLEY (*stopping in some dismay*) Where's Mr Hathaway—do you know?
GEORGE (*busy with the lamp*) No, I don't, I'm afraid.

(WEMBLEY *makes an exasperated sound*)

WEMBLEY (*turning away*) Oh, dear! What a morning!
GEORGE (*suddenly thinking of something*) Oh—Mr Wembley . . .

(WEMBLEY *exits up* C)

(*He turns*) Where's Waldorf? (*He realizes Wembley has gone*)

(WALDORF *enters by the alcove up* R)

WALDORF (*with a friendly smile*) I'm here.
GEORGE (*turning; startled*) Oh!
WALDORF. I thought I heard one of my names.
GEORGE (*a little embarrassed*) Yes, I—expect you heard one or two other things as well.
WALDORF. No, I'm afraid not.

(GEORGE *looks relieved*)

I've been speaking to Belgravia and Jubilee. (*He crosses to* LC)
GEORGE. To who?
WALDORF. Some dummies I know. But they couldn't answer me at all.
GEORGE. Hardly. (*He glances purposefully from Waldorf to the lamp, then moves a chair from* LC *and sets it near the lamp*)
WALDORF. I'm in a different world now, you see.
GEORGE. Yes. (*He focuses the lamp on the chair*) I suppose you are for the moment. I expect you're a bit homesick for the other one, really? (*He smiles hopefully at Waldorf*)
WALDORF. No—not really. Not at all.
GEORGE (*his hopeful smile fading*) Oh. (*With some significance*) Of course, you haven't seen much of this one yet, have you?
WALDORF (*happily*) I've seen the National Insurance office. That was beautiful.
GEORGE. Yes—well, of course, it doesn't all come up to that.
WALDORF. I suppose not.

(GEORGE, *somewhat taken aback, sits for a moment on the chair to check the focus of the lamp*)

GEORGE (*with a friendly smile*) Pity—from your point of view—that your—er—little accident should just have happened at a time like this.
WALDORF. Oh, I'm enjoying the Sale, too.
GEORGE. I was thinking of life in general. When you think of the international situation, and the cost of living and the housing problem . . . Do you know the population is going up by over two thousand five hundred every week?
WALDORF (*happily*) It's gone up by one this morning.
GEORGE (*grimly*) Yes. And what's the result? (*He moves the second chair and sets it beside the other near the lamp*) Crime is on the increase, six out of every ten marriages end in divorce and traffic in the West End is almost at a standstill. (*He indicates the first chair*) Shall we?
WALDORF (*eyeing George a little curiously; politely*) Thank you—very much. (*He crosses and sits on the first chair*)

(GEORGE, *delighted at the success of his manoeuvres so far, sits on the second chair*)

GEORGE. Look at the public services, look at purchase tax, look at the weather.

(WALDORF *looks vaguely around in various directions*)

Nothing's what it used to be, and never will be again. Go out to work, and every penny you're paid goes in Take What You Earn. And when you get home in the evening, what have you got? The B.B.C. and the I.T.V. And both of those are N.B.G. (*He rises, goes to the lamp to adjusts it*)

(MISS BUTTERWORTH *enters up* C. *She is a cheerful, tough and extremely well-built girl.* WALDORF's *eyes light up at the sight of her and he rises*)

MISS BUTTERWORTH (*with a brisk smile*) Excuse me—(*she moves down* C) you haven't by any chance seen Mr Hathaway?
GEORGE (*ferociously*) No—we haven't.
MISS BUTTERWORTH. Oh! (*She sees Waldorf*) Oh!

(MISS BUTTERWORTH, *her hips swaying a little, exits up* C)

WALDORF (*moving up* C) Who was that?
GEORGE (*busy with the lamp; abstractedly*) One of the old man's secretaries. Take it from me, old man, life isn't worth living—it isn't really.
WALDORF (*gazing at the exit up* C) I'm sorry you feel like that.
GEORGE (*busy with the lamp*) Everybody feels like that. Anybody would far sooner be a wax dummy.
WALDORF (*moving to the exit up* C; *his hips swaying like Miss Butterworth's*) Good-bye.
GEORGE. Well, it won't be quite yet . . . (*He looks at Waldorf. Startled*) What?
WALDORF (*with a charming smile*) Personally, *I'm* finding life delightful.

(WALDORF *exits purposefully up* C, *in pursuit of Miss Butterworth*)

GEORGE (*agitatedly*) Hey—no! (*He turns to follow Waldorf, only to find his ankle entwined in the flex. He struggles exasperatedly to free himself*)

(WEMBLEY *enters up* C, *and moves down* C. *He looks still more agitated*)

WEMBLEY (*in desperation*) I've *got* to find Mr Hathaway somewhere—will you please come and . . . (*Exasperated*) Ingle! Really! Are you *still* fiddling about with that?
GEORGE (*freeing himself*) Mr Wembley—I think I can fix

everything. I suddenly thought. (*He switches on the lamp, which glows red*) The infra red.
WEMBLEY (*almost beside himself*) Oh, for heaven's sake! (*He turns despairingly away*)

(HATHAWAY *enters up* C. *He looks a little fussed, but is beginning to get over it*)

(*Relieved*) Mr Hathaway . . .
HATHAWAY. I hear he's been found—and about time, too. (*He looks blankly around*) Where is he? (*He moves down* RC)
GEORGE (*swallowing slightly*) He's gone again, sir.
HATHAWAY (*outraged*) What!
GEORGE. You see, sir, I suddenly thought of something . . .
WEMBLEY. Ingle! Please! What I have to say is urgent. Mr Hathaway, I really must lodge a protest—if Miss Yates is going to do this sort of thing, how *can* we all pull together?
HATHAWAY (*impatiently*) What sort of thing?
WEMBLEY. She's marking things down, all over her departments.
HATHAWAY (*moving down* R; *exasperated*) There happens to be a Sale, Wembley.
WEMBLEY. But she's marking down from the mark down prices.
HATHAWAY. She's what?
WEMBLEY. By pounds, Mr Hathaway, in some cases. A lot of the special bargain lines will be only just above the ordinary figure.
HATHAWAY. But that's outrageous!
WEMBLEY. That's what *I* think, Mr Hathaway. D'you know what she's done at the glove counter?

(*At each new price* WEMBLEY *moves* L, *showing with a gesture sections of a counter.* HATHAWAY *moves with him*)

Moved all the sixty-three shilling into the forty-five-and-six tray, all the forty-five-and-six into the twenty-three-and-eleven and so on, right down to the cottons at four-and-sixpence halfpenny!
HATHAWAY (*gaping*) Where's she moved those?
WEMBLEY. Off the counter altogether and down to the bargain basement. Naturally, you can't get near them! And look how it's going to reflect on my departments.
HATHAWAY. She must have gone out of her mind.
WEMBLEY. That's exactly what I told her—my very words. She just laughed in my face. (*He imitates Miss Yates' laugh*) D'you know what she said? She said it's taken a dummy to put some sense into her.
HATHAWAY. A dummy?
GEORGE. Sir, if I could suggest something . . .

(WEMBLEY *glares at George*)

WEMBLEY (*to Hathaway*) What she meant, sir, I don't know.
HATHAWAY (*grimly*) We'll very soon find out. (*He moves to the exit up* C)

(WEMBLEY *follows Hathaway to the exit.*
The DOORMAN *enters up* C. *He looks hot and bothered*)

DOORMAN (*to Hathaway*) Excuse me, sir—there's a lot of trouble going on with Oakshott.
HATHAWAY (*exasperated*) Oh, for God's sake. What kind of trouble?
DOORMAN. It's the shoplifters, sir. They're out in force, as you might suppose, and she was doing fine early on. Now, all of a sudden she's turning a blind eye. She's just winking at it, sir.
HATHAWAY (*confused*) Winking—with a blind eye? What are you talking about?
DOORMAN. She won't put a finger on one of 'em, sir. She's letting them walk away with it.

(HATHAWAY *moves down* C)

(*He moves to* R *of Hathaway*) There's two women went out the door not a minute ago—

(HATHAWAY *crosses to* LC)

—(*he moves to* R *of Hathaway*) one with her muff full of potted shrimps and the other——

(HATHAWAY *crosses to* RC)

—(*he moves to* L *of Hathaway*) with a pair of roller skates stuffed up her sweater—complete with ball bearings.
HATHAWAY. Oh! Disgusting!
DOORMAN. And not a wrapping in sight.
HATHAWAY. Someone should have found Oakshott—told her.
DOORMAN. She's been told half a dozen times, sir, she won't even listen. Mr Fortescue tackled her, in Dress Materials. All she said was—she understood now, about temptation. That, and something about this Waldorf.
HATHAWAY. Waldorf!
GEORGE. In both cases.
WEMBLEY (*moving down* LC) It's havoc, Mr Hathaway, that's what it is.
DOORMAN (*to Hathaway*) There's sixteen scarves missing, too, and a whole counterful of costume jewellery.
HATHAWAY. What! (*To the Doorman and Wembley*) Find Oakshott and Miss Yates—tell them I want to see them immediately.
WEMBLEY. Yes, Mr Hathaway. (*He moves up* C)
DOORMAN. Yes, sir. (*He moves up* C)
HATHAWAY. And if we can't talk some sense into Oakshott

we'll call in a constable, off the beat. And above all, we have to find that dummy—lock him up somewhere.

(WEMBLEY *and the* DOORMAN *exit hurriedly up* C. HATHAWAY *moves to the exit up* C)

GEORGE (*desperately*) Mr Hathaway—if you *please*, sir . . .
HATHAWAY (*stopping and turning; impatiently*) What is it?
GEORGE. I know what to do about him, sir, I'm sure. I believe we can put an end to the trouble once and for all.
HATHAWAY (*desperately*) I'd give a lot to know how.
GEORGE. With the lamp, sir. It suddenly came over me. If the ultra violet was a bit too ultra, and that's what brought him to life, how about the infra red?
HATHAWAY. How about it?
GEORGE. Ten to one, that's a bit too infra. It's the opposite end of the spectrum. Ten to one, it would have the opposite effect.
HATHAWAY. You mean . . . ?
GEORGE. Yes, sir.
HATHAWAY (*after a moment*) It's certainly worth trying.
GEORGE. That's what I mean, sir. The only thing is, we've got to keep him in range, so to speak, long enough to give the thing a chance to . . . (*He breaks off*)

(WALDORF, *calm and unruffled, strolls in up* C. HATHAWAY *and* GEORGE *both stiffen*)

WALDORF (*with one of his charming smiles*) Excuse me. (*He moves to the chairs down* LC *and removes the carrier bag*)
HATHAWAY (*quietly, but not in an undertone; to George*) You can—leave that side of the matter to me.
GEORGE (*tensely*) O.K., Mr Hathaway. (*He moves down* L)

(WALDORF, *having picked up the bag, is about to go*)

HATHAWAY (*to Waldorf; genially*) My dear fellow—I've been hoping for a word with you. Come and sit down. (*He eases Waldorf towards the chairs down* L)
WALDORF (*with a polite smile*) Thank you very much, but I can't stay—because of the colour. (*He turns to go*)

(HATHAWAY *and* GEORGE *exchange glances, with a look at the lamp*)

HATHAWAY (*rather sharply*) Colour? What d'you mean?
WALDORF. She's waiting for me—to bring it out. (*He turns to go*)
HATHAWAY (*restraining Waldorf*) Look—er—don't worry about that. I'll—er—come with you afterwards and help you do it.

(GEORGE *puts the chair* L *against the wall* L, *and re-positions the remaining chair in the focus of the lamp*)

ACT II MAN ALIVE 55

WALDORF (*looking at Hathaway*) Oh, no, thank you—I wouldn't care for that. (*He turns to go*)
HATHAWAY (*anxiously*) But, just a minute, there's something very important. It—er—it concerns your whole future.

(WALDORF *stops and turns*)

(*Impressively*) I've been thinking over the matter and in view of your—er—(*he eases Waldorf down* LC) very exceptional knowledge, I propose to offer you the post of deputy chairman of the company.
WALDORF (*vaguely*) Deputy chairman?
GEORGE. It means thousands a year.
WALDORF (*interested at last*) Thousands of women?
HATHAWAY (*exasperated*) Pounds.

(WALDORF, *promptly losing interest again, shrugs and turns to go*)

GEORGE (*hurriedly*) But it comes to the same thing.
WALDORF (*stopping and turning*) Does it?

(GEORGE *crosses to* R *of Waldorf*)

HATHAWAY. Of course it does. (*He takes his cigar case from his pocket. Expansively*) You'll have a free hand. (*He offers the case to Waldorf*) Cigar?
WALDORF (*taking a cigar*) Thank you very much.
GEORGE (*taking the carrier from Waldorf*) Allow me. (*He crosses and puts the carrier on the dressing-table*)

(HATHAWAY *takes a cigar for himself and puts his case in his pocket*)

WALDORF (*indicating the sun-lamp*) That's a nice colour, too. (*He eats the cigar*)
HATHAWAY. Yes. We think so. As a matter of fact . . . (*He breaks off as he sees that Waldorf is eating the cigar*)

(GEORGE *moves* C, *sees Hathaway staring, looks at Waldorf, and gapes*)

WALDORF (*with a friendly smile*) Quite different from a rum sundae.

(GEORGE *crosses above the other two and stands down* L)

HATHAWAY (*swallowing slightly*) Yes—I should think it would be.
WALDORF (*in a tone of concern*) You're not having yours.

(HATHAWAY *almost automatically takes a bite of his cigar, then splutters*)

HATHAWAY. I—don't feel quite like it at the moment. (*He puts the cigar in his pocket*) As I was saying—we were just trying out a new effect for the window—but we can't get on, because we haven't a dummy. (*Hastily*) A—er—wax figure, perhaps I should say.

WALDORF (*as he finishes the cigar*) Like *I* used to be? (*He sucks his fingers*)

HATHAWAY. Quite. I mean—happy as we are to have you with us—in your new capacity—delighted, in fact—we shall, of course, have to replace you.

(WALDORF *wipes his fingers on the front of Hathaway's suit*)

(*He restrains himself with difficulty*) I wonder! I suppose you wouldn't—just while we're waiting—be very kind and model for us yourself?

GEORGE. Just so we can try out the effect.

HATHAWAY (*frowning at George a little*) Quite. (*Casually*) It's the sort of thing a deputy chairman is usually happy to do. So—will you—(*he manages an uneasy smile*) Waldorf?

WALDORF. Certainly.

HATHAWAY (*delighted and relieved*) Thank you very much indeed. (*He sits on the chair near the lamp*)

GEORGE (*to Waldorf*) Just stand over here—if you don't mind. (*He manoeuvres Waldorf to a position* L *of and not far from Hathaway*)

WALDORF (*posing*) Like this?

HATHAWAY. That's fine. (*To George*) Isn't it?

GEORGE. I think it will be, sir—all in good time. (*He changes the direction of the lamp, so that the red glow falls on Waldorf*)

(HATHAWAY, *in his chair, is close by*)

(*To Hathaway*) How's that, sir?

HATHAWAY. Promising. Distinctly promising. Now—let's just see one or two things. Try those grey flannels, over there . . .

WALDORF. Me? (*He takes a step towards the alcove up* L)

HATHAWAY (*hurriedly*) No, no—you stay where you are. Don't move. (*He rises, puts Waldorf into his place, then resumes his seat*)

(GEORGE *moves to the alcove up* L *and collects the flannels.*

WEMBLEY, *breathless but triumphant, enters up* C *and moves down* C)

WEMBLEY. They've both been told, Mr Hathaway.

HATHAWAY (*without moving; tersely*) Go away.

WEMBLEY. I beg your pardon, Mr Hathaway?

HATHAWAY (*angrily*) Go away. Can't you see I'm busy?

WEMBLEY. Yes, sir, I—(*he stares at Waldorf*) I see you are.

HATHAWAY (*caustically*) Since you have not provided a new figure for the window, our friend, Mr—er . . .

WALDORF (*bowing*) Patent-Pending.

HATHAWAY. Quite. (*To Wembley*) . . . is very kindly doing duty for one.

ACT II   MAN ALIVE   57

WALDORF (*to Wembley*) It's the sort of thing a deputy chairman is usually happy to do.
WEMBLEY (*puzzled*) I beg your . . . ?
HATHAWAY (*hastily*) Mr Pending is the new deputy chairman of the company.
WEMBLEY (*thunderstruck*) The new . . .
HATHAWAY (*abruptly*) And that will be all, thank you, Wembley.
WEMBLEY (*gaping*) Very good, Mr Hathaway. I'll fetch a new dummy in straightaway. (*He turns to go*)
HATHAWAY (*sharply*) No, no—don't do that. You'd better go and look out a suitable wardrobe. Something preparatory for the coming season.

(WEMBLEY *moves to the exit up* C)

And take your time.
WEMBLEY (*completely crushed*) Yes, Mr Hathaway.

(WEMBLEY *exits up* C. WALDORF *blows him a kiss*. GEORGE *moves to Waldorf and drapes the flannels over his arm*)

HATHAWAY (*to George*) No—I don't care for that.

(GEORGE *removes the flannels*)

GEORGE (*crossing above Waldorf to* R *of him*) Not getting stiff, I hope?
WALDORF. No, thank you.
GEORGE (*with a glance at Hathaway*) Don't worry, sir. I'm sure we shall arrive at it sooner or later. (*He moves to the alcove up* L) I'll just try the blazer. (*He picks up the blazer and drapes it over Waldorf's arm*) How about that, sir?

(HATHAWAY *seems about to speak, then just shakes his head, rather stiffly*)

(*He shakes his head*) No, sir? (*He moves to* L *of Waldorf*) Well, maybe a cardigan. (*He discards the blazer and tries one of the cardigans*)
WALDORF (*still holding his pose*) Will it be long?
GEORGE. Can't really say. Just depends when we get the effect we're looking for. Something the matter?
WALDORF. No, I just feel a little strange.

(*The transition sound is heard*)

GEORGE (*trying to conceal his delight*) You do? Well, I don't think it'll be too long. (*He grins at Hathaway and tries another cardigan*) No. No good, is it, sir? I'll see if there's something in there.
WALDORF (*still motionless*) Perhaps it was the cigar.
GEORGE (*cheerfully*) I expect so. You shouldn't have eaten it

with the band on. (*He goes into the alcove up* L *with the clothes and puts them on the bed*)

WALDORF (*still holding his pose*) I am beginning to feel stiff, too, Mr Hathaway.

(HATHAWAY *does not reply*)

Do you think I could move just a little ? Just for a moment?

(HATHAWAY *does not reply*)

Mr Hathaway—Mr Hathaway! (*He leans forward a little to look at Hathaway and touches his shoulder*)

(HATHAWAY *leans forward a little, like a dummy. The transition sound ceases*)

(*He moves behind Hathaway, puts him straight, then calls blithely*) Ingle.
  GEORGE (*moving excitedly to* L *of Hathaway*) Something happened. sir?
  WALDORF. I think it has.
  GEORGE (*turning in surprise*) What!
  WALDORF (*with a gesture*) To Mr Hathaway.

(GEORGE *turns to Hathaway*)

He doesn't seem to answer.

(HATHAWAY *sits motionless in his chair, a fixed expression on his face*)

  GEORGE (*anxiously*) What is it, Mr Hathaway? (*He moves closer to Hathaway*) Mr Hathaway ... (*He stares in alarm*) Mr Hath ... (*He looks aghast at Hathaway, then looks at the lamp. Realization and dismay overwhelm him*) Oh, my holy Aunt Christina!
  WALDORF. He looks a little strange. And he didn't have *his* cigar.

(GEORGE *pats Hathaway's hands and rubs them to try and restore the circulation*)

  GEORGE. Mr Hathaway—*please*, Mr Hathaway. (*Desperately*) Say something. (*He raises Hathaway's arms*)
  WALDORF. You know what *I* think?
  GEORGE (*frantically*) I know. I know. Don't rub it in. (*Desperately*) Oh, for heaven's sake! (*He lifts Hathaway's legs and they stick straight out*) Stiff as a poker. (*He moans*) Oh, what am I going to do now? (*He puts Hathaway's arms and legs down and looks wildly around. Suddenly his eye falls again on the lamp. He thinks of something and his face brightens*) Don't worry, Mr Hathaway—just a little accident—just temporary, that's all. I'll have you right in a jiffy. I'm going to switch it over to U.V. (*He dashes to the lamp*)

ACT II   MAN ALIVE

(OAKSHOTT *enters breezily up* C. WALDORF *stares interestedly at Hathaway, masking him from Oakshott*)

OAKSHOTT. Mr Hathaway here? (*She moves to the dressing-table and picks up her handbag*)

(GEORGE *hastily picks up a dust sheet from the corner down* L *and throws it over Hathaway*)

GEORGE. No—he isn't.

(GEORGE *hurriedly propels Hathaway in the chair and exits with him to the alcove up* L, *closing the curtains behind them*)

OAKSHOTT (*smiling warmly*) Hullo, Wal. (*She crosses to Waldorf*)

(WALDORF *smiles at Oakshott*)

Where is he, Wal, do you know?
WALDORF. He just went out.

(MISS YATES *enters up* C *and moves down* RC)

MISS YATES (*looking around*) Mr Hathaway?
OAKSHOTT. Not here, apparently.
MISS YATES. Where's he gone? Did he say?
WALDORF. No—he didn't.

(*The* DOORMAN *enters up* C)

DOORMAN. Where's the guv'nor?
WALDORF. Not here.

(*The* DOORMAN *crosses to the lamp down* L, *unplugs it and picks it up*)

MISS YATES (*to Oakshott*) Oh, well, if *you* see him, let me know in the stockroom.

(MISS YATES *smiles warmly at Waldorf and exits up* C)

OAKSHOTT (*with a shrug*) I expect he's over it by now, anyway.

(OAKSHOTT *smiles at Waldorf and exits up* C)

DOORMAN. Despatch have come for this. Just tell Mr Hathaway it's gone all right, will you?
WALDORF (*with a friendly smile*) Certainly.
DOORMAN (*moving to the exit up* C) I expect even so, he'll have something to say about it.
WALDORF. I don't think he will.
DOORMAN (*with a grin*) You don't know the guv'nor.
WALDORF. You wouldn't know him, if you saw him now.

(*The* DOORMAN *exits with the lamp up* C. GEORGE *peers out of the alcove up* L)

GEORGE. All clear?
WALDORF. I beg your pardon?
GEORGE (*peering around the curtain; urgently*) Have they gone?
WALDORF. Oh, yes. All of them. (*He moves to the table up* LC *and examines the things on it*)

(GEORGE, *relieved, parts the curtains and pushes out the chair, in which* HATHAWAY *is still seated, covered with the dust sheet*)

GEORGE (*pushing the chair down* LC) Don't worry, Mr Hathaway, won't be a minute now. (*He removes the dust sheet*) I'll have you O.K. in no time. (*He looks down* L. *In dismay*) Where's the lamp?
WALDORF (*with a charming smile*) That's gone, too. (*He picks up an inkpad and rubber stamp and moves towards Hathaway*)
GEORGE (*aghast*) What! Where? Who?
WALDORF. Despatch, I think he said.
GEORGE (*wailing*) Oh, my long suffering uncles! (*He dashes towards the exit up* C)

(*The* DOORMAN *enters up* C. *He carries a slip of paper*)

DOORMAN (*holding out the slip*) Receipt.

(GEORGE *takes the slip of paper*)

GEORGE (*gaping*) Pat—have they . . . ?
DOORMAN. Yes—van's just gone.

(*The* DOORMAN *smiles cheerfully and exits up* C. GEORGE *stares in horror at the receipt*)

WALDORF (*looking at Hathaway*) I thought he wouldn't say anything.
GEORGE (*desperately*) I'll have to ring the people—tell 'em to send it straight back.

(WALDORF *bends Hathaway forward in the chair*)

Hey—what are you doing?
WALDORF. Just going to put his name on. (*He breathes on the rubber stamp and applies it to the ink pad*)

(GEORGE *moves quickly to Waldorf and snatches the stamp from him*)

GEORGE (*horror-struck*) Don't you *dare*! (*He glances at the stamp and reads*) "Hathaway's—received with thanks." Certainly *not*! (*He pulls Hathaway to an upright position. Agitatedly*) I *beg* your pardon, Mr Hathaway . . .

GEORGE *is still apologizing as*—

the CURTAIN *falls*

ACT III

SCENE—*The same. Half an hour later.*
The chaise is now C. *The two chairs are set, one* R *of the exit up* C *and one against the wall* L. *On the chair* R *of the exit there is a maternity smock, a long white wedding dress and a bridal veil. The curtains of both alcoves are closed. The window has been tidied. The lighting is for* "*blind down*".

When the CURTAIN *rises,* WALDORF *and* MISS BUTTERWORTH *are seated on the chaise, in a warm embrace, Waldorf* L *of Miss Butterworth. After a moment they emerge from the embrace.*

MISS BUTTERWORTH. I really *must* find Mr Hathaway. (*She attempts to rise*)
WALDORF (*restraining her*) There's no immediate hurry, is there?
MISS BUTTERWORTH (*looking at him, large-eyed*) Are you a wolf! You told me if I came in here, I wouldn't need to look any further.
WALDORF. Well, do you? (*He kisses her again, even more warmly*)
MISS BUTTERWORTH (*a little breathless*) How long have you been working here?
WALDORF. Since this morning. How long have you?
MISS BUTTERWORTH. Well—I used to be a model, actually.
WALDORF (*surprised*) You were?

(MISS BUTTERWORTH *nods*)

What sort of accident did *you* have?
MISS BUTTERWORTH (*a shade indignantly*) It wasn't an accident. Mr Hathaway promoted me on my merits.
WALDORF (*enthusiastically*) I like them, too. (*He puts an arm around her and kisses her with considerable passion*) Have a cigar?
MISS BUTTERWORTH (*startled*) What?

(WALDORF *produces Hathaway's cigar case and offers it*)

(*She stares at the case*) That's Mr Hathaway's.
WALDORF. Yes—that's right.
MISS BUTTERWORTH. Did he lose it?
WALDORF (*blithely*) Yes—he did. Won't you—they're delicious.
MISS BUTTERWORTH (*taking the case*) Yes—I think I'd better. I'll see he gets it back, as soon as possible.
WALDORF (*a little taken aback*) Oh. (*He thinks of something else*) Well, have one of these. (*He takes a handful of costume jewellery from his pocket and holds it out to her*)

Miss Butterworth (*astonished*) What! What's all that?
Waldorf. Costume jewellery, I think they call it. Shall I put some on *your* costume?
Miss Butterworth (*in some alarm*) Thank you—I think not. (*She looks curiously at him*) What department are you in?
Waldorf (*pocketing the jewellery*) I've no idea. Furniture, I suppose it would be.
Miss Butterworth. Furniture?
Waldorf. I'm the deputy chairman.
Miss Butterworth (*aghast*) What! (*She jumps up, as though stung. Slightly aggrieved*) Mr Hathaway never told anyone.
Waldorf. I shan't tell anyone, if they're going to do that every time. Come and sit down.
Miss Butterworth (*eyeing him*) I suppose Mr H is very much elsewhere?
Waldorf. Not very much. (*He indicates the alcove up* L) He's in there.
Miss Butterworth (*looking at him in mock exasperation*) Just a great big tease, aren't you? Oh, well, I suppose you'll be handling a lot of the nonsense yourself now?
Waldorf (*rising*) I'm trying to handle anything I can. (*He moves to her*) Why don't you come and sit down?

(Miss Butterworth *puts a hand on Waldorf's chest to make him keep his distance*)

Miss Butterworth (*dryly*) Work, I was referring to. There's a pile waiting up in the office—trading returns for last week, rating amendments from the Borough Council and God knows what—I don't know which you'd like to start with.
Waldorf. I don't think I'd like any of those.
Miss Butterworth. Well, you'll have to start with something, won't you?
Waldorf. What would *you* start with?
Miss Butterworth. If I were deputy chairman?

(Waldorf *nods*)

A bottle of champagne, probably.
Waldorf (*brightly*) Then, that's what I'll start with.
Miss Butterworth (*looking at him, amused*) Want me to have one opened—from the Wine Department?
Waldorf. Have they got one?
Miss Butterworth (*giving him a look*) Only about two thousand.
Waldorf. Have them all opened. (*He moves above the chaise*)
Miss Butterworth (*astounded*) All?
Waldorf. Why not?
Miss Butterworth. There'd be enough for everyone in the store.

WALDORF. There would?

(MISS BUTTERWORTH *nods*)

Good.
MISS BUTTERWORTH (*with growing amazement*) You aren't serious are you?
WALDORF. Why not?
MISS BUTTERWORTH. You mean—champagne all round?
WALDORF. Champagne all round.
MISS BUTTERWORTH. But there's a Sale on—what are the customers going to say?
WALDORF. "Yes, please", I expect. (*He moves below the chaise, sits and pats the seat beside him, for her to sit again*)

(MISS BUTTERWORTH *stares at him in astonishment*.
WEMBLEY *enters up* C. *He carries an armful of scarlet and grey clothes. We cannot see exactly what they are*)

WEMBLEY (*moving* C; *vexedly*) Mr Hathaway gone again? Oh, dear! (*He turns to go*)
MISS BUTTERWORTH (*with a step towards Wembley*) Mr Wembley... (*To Waldorf*) Of course, you don't really mean it, do you? In fact, you aren't really at all, are you?
WALDORF (*puzzled*) I beg your pardon?
MISS BUTTERWORTH. Mr Wembley—did you hear anything? About a new deputy chairman?
WEMBLEY (*with a frigid glance at Waldorf*) Mr Hathaway told me. (*Acidly*) Don't ask me to explain the appointment. I can't. (*He puts the clothes on the chaise*)
MISS BUTTERWORTH. I've got no complaints. (*She smiles warmly at Waldorf*)
WALDORF (*gravely*) He said I have a free hand.
MISS BUTTERWORTH. I can believe *that*. It's going to cost a packet, but what publicity. I'll go straight along and start things popping. (*She moves to the exit up* C *then stops and turns. To Waldorf*) You did say every bottle?
WALDORF. Why not?
MISS BUTTERWORTH. Wow! What a boozy little old party this is going to be.

(MISS BUTTERWORTH *exits up* C)

WALDORF (*indicating the clothing*) Is that something preparatory for the coming season?
WEMBLEY (*irritably*) Yes—yes. (*He picks up the clothing*) Has Ingle disappeared, too?
WALDORF. Yes, but not in the same way.
WEMBLEY (*moving towards the alcove up* L) Really, if it isn't one thing this morning, it's another.

(DAPHNE *enters up* C *and moves towards the alcove up* R)

Miss Jameson—where's Ingle, do you know?

DAPHNE (*beaming at Waldorf*) I've no idea at all. I haven't seen him for half an hour at least.

(DAPHNE *exits backwards through the curtains into the alcove up* R)

WEMBLEY (*agitatedly*) Half an hour—and no new dummy.

WALDORF. Oh, yes, there is.

WEMBLEY (*surprised*) Where?

WALDORF (*indicating the alcove up* L) In there. (*He rises and moves up* L. *With a helpful smile*) Shall I show you?

WEMBLEY (*impatiently*) Thank you, but I've rather more important matters to attend to. (*Exasperatedly*) Now I suppose I shall have to go looking for Ingle—in the meantime, of course, he'll come back here.

WALDORF. Is there anything I can do? As deputy chairman?

WEMBLEY (*indicating the clothing*) These are to go on it, at the earliest possible moment.

WALDORF. Allow me. (*He takes the clothing from Wembley*)

WEMBLEY. And then, of course, it's to come out here. I want it displayed to the very best advantage. Is that clear?

WALDORF. Oh—quite. (*He moves to the alcove up* L)

WEMBLEY. And kindly tell Ingle to be as quick as he can. The longer Mr Hathaway has to wait for anything, the angrier he gets.

WALDORF. He won't have to wait long for these.

(WALDORF *smiles reassuringly and exits by the alcove up* L. WEMBLEY, *sighs, turns, and still full of vexation, moves towards the exit up* C.

MISS YATES *enters up* C. *She carries three straw hats and a spray of apple blossom. She is humming cheerfully to herself. Her personality has acquired a new lightness and gaiety*)

MISS YATES (*moving to* R *of Wembley*) Hullo, Wembley—how's *your* Happy New Year?

WEMBLEY (*exceedingly frigid*) It is *not*.

MISS YATES (*gaily*) Oh, but it should be. (*She tickles his chin with the blossom, then moves above the chaise and puts the hats and blossom on it*)

WEMBLEY (*acidly*) I can't stop. Thanks to Oakshott, there's a crisis at the Help Yourself Cap Counter. Customers are taking the notice literally.

(WEMBLEY *glares at Miss Yates, then exits up* C. MISS YATES *looks after him, amused, then she turns towards the alcove up* R)

MISS YATES (*calling blithely*) Daphne.

(DAPHNE's *head appears through the curtains of the alcove up* R)

DAPHNE (*in a tone of surprise*) Do you mean me, Miss Yates?

Miss Yates (*smiling*) Who else would I mean? Are they ready?
Daphne (*brightly*) Just finishing. (*She withdraws her head*)

(Miss Yates *looks appraisingly at the hats, humming to herself.*
Oakshott *enters up* c. *She, too, has undergone a change of personality under the impact of Waldorf. She is decidedly skittish*)

Oakshott (*moving* LC) Still not here? Old push-cart, I mean.
Miss Yates. If you're referring to Mr Hathaway—the old push-cart hasn't wheeled his way into *my* view since he sent for me. And I couldn't care less.
Oakshott. Can't think where he's got to. I've been looking all over the shop. Literally.

(Fred *carries* Belgravia *in by the alcove up* R *and stands her down* LC. *She is attired in striped drainpipe slacks and a striped off-the-shoulder blouse*)

Oh, I say! (*She looks admiringly at Belgravia's outfit*)

(Fred *exits up* c)

Belgravia (*bitterly*) The things I do for Oxford Street.
Oakshott (*crossing below Belgravia to* c) I like that. (*To Miss Yates*) I wonder how it would look on me.
Belgravia. Disastrous.

(Miss Yates *picks up a hat and moves to Belgravia*)

Oakshott. Is that the hat?
Miss Yates. That's the hat. (*She puts the hat on Belgravia*)
Oakshott (*looking at the hats on the chaise*) I don't know why, but I feel like a new hat this morning.
Belgravia. You look like an old hat, same as any other morning.

(Daphne *wheels* Jubilee *on by the alcove up* R. Jubilee *is dressed in blue jeans and is seated astride a bright red tricycle, which has a toy rabbit in the basket on the handlebars*)

Jubilee. I really think at my age, this is asking too much.

(Miss Yates *moves to the chaise and picks up the apple blossom.*
Oakshott *moves up* c *and looks at the wedding dress and maternity smock*)

Belgravia (*bitterly*) With Yates in her present mood—girlish heart all a-flutter—you're lucky not to be airborne, with wings and a bow and arrow.
Daphne. Whereabouts, Miss Yates?
Miss Yates (*moving to Belgravia*) Down here, near the other one. (*She indicates a position* L *of Belgravia*)

(Daphne *wheels Jubilee* L *of Belgravia*)

I want to suggest a walk in the park—in spring-time. (*She puts the blossom in Belgravia's right hand*)
BELGRAVIA. With a bedroom suite in the background? Now I *know* she's off her head.
JUBILEE. Love does strange things to a woman.
BELGRAVIA. That's no excuse for her doing strange things to us. And talk about change her mind—it was a toss-up whether I'd be an expectant mother, a bride, or this.

(MISS YATES *adjusts Belgravia's outfit.* DAPHNE *adjusts Jubilee's outfit*)

OAKSHOTT (*indicating the smock and dress*) I don't think either of these is quite me—not till someone proposes, anyway. (*She moves down* C *with the garments*) But *that* one. (*She looks admiringly at Belgravia's outfit*) If old push-cart sacks me, as I fully expect, I'll probably buy it and wear it on duty for the rest of the week. That'll show him how much *I* care.

(OAKSHOTT *replaces the clothes on the chair, then exits up* C. DAPHNE *looks after her, a little wonderingly*)

MISS YATES (*happily*) I know just how she feels. As a matter of fact, I think Mr Hathaway is probably going to sack me too. (*She steps back from Belgravia and Jubilee and looks appraisingly at them*) There! (*She moves to the chaise and picks up the hats*) If he doesn't like that, he can do the other thing. Now, let's go and do our worst in the way of accessories.

(DAPHNE *stares at Miss Yates*)

What's the matter with you, Daphne?
DAPHNE. Nothing, Miss Yates. You both seem different, that's all.
MISS YATES. Different?
DAPHNE. You and Oakshott. (*With sudden realization and a happy smile*) But, of course, it's only me, really.

(MISS YATES *laughs and gaily plomps one hat on Daphne's head and the other on her own. They both look ridiculous.*)

DAPHNE *exits up* C.
MISS YATES *follows her off. There is a moment of silence*)

JUBILEE. Well! He seems to be quite Waldorf the Conqueror, doesn't he?
BELGRAVIA. I am more disgusted than ever with the sex to which we have the appearance of belonging.
JUBILEE. You really did take a fancy to Waldorf, didn't you?

(BELGRAVIA *does not answer*)

Now, come along, dear—you know what they say—a trouble shared is a trouble halved. It's true now, isn't it?

Act III   MAN ALIVE   67

BELGRAVIA (*resignedly*) All right—if it'll make you any happier. The moment I set eyes on him, I said to myself, "There's the one dummy I could cheerfully share the same window with, till the day we're both melted down". A fine hope of that, now.

JUBILEE. I quite thought, from what one could hear, that we were going to have him with us again. What went wrong, do you suppose?

BELGRAVIA. If it's what it sounded to be, I should describe it as poetic justice.

JUBILEE. You don't really think that poor Mr Hathaway . . . Ho! Ho! Ho! Dear, oh, dear!

BELGRAVIA. If he has, it's the one thing that'll save my day from utter ruin. (*She sighs*)

JUBILEE (*brightly*) Come, come now—chin up.

BELGRAVIA. Don't be ridiculous—I can only move when I'm moved.

JUBILEE. I'm sure it will all come right in the end. True love always does.

BELGRAVIA (*dryly*) I suppose no-one ever told you about Romeo and Juliet, or Tristan and Isolde, or Antony and Cleopatra?

JUBILEE (*pensively*) I don't think they did. Let me see. I know Dickins and Jones, and Bourne and Hollingsworth.

BELGRAVIA. Those are not in quite the same category.

JUBILEE. What category is that?

BELGRAVIA. Beautiful but indescribably sad. They came to a tragic end, every one of them.

JUBILEE. Oh—like Stag and Mantle.

BELGRAVIA (*giving up*) Have it your own way.

(*The* DOORMAN *enters up* C *and stands to one side.*

MISS ADSHEAD *enters up* C. *She is a brisk, eager, mannish woman in the thirties. She wears a duffle-coat*)

DOORMAN (*a little baffled*) Nobody here at all, now. But if it's all that urgent, you're more likely here than anywhere else.

MISS ADSHEAD (*moving below the chaise*) It's very urgent indeed. Will you just tell him I'm from Olux Lamps.

DOORMAN. I'll try what I can. Information may know something—but I doubt it.

(*The* DOORMAN *exits up* C. MISS ADSHEAD *looks around and takes a rather disgusted look at Belgravia and Jubilee. She moves between them and looks at Belgravia*)

JUBILEE. What is it, dear—a man or a woman?

(MISS ADSHEAD *turns and examines the rabbit in the basket of the tricycle*)

BELGRAVIA. I should think the top half is one and the bottom the other.

(Miss ADSHEAD *crosses to the chaise*)

Not that it can matter much.

(Miss ADSHEAD *sits on the chaise and waits, staring out front. She is as motionless as the other two.*

WALDORF *enters by the alcove up* L, *carrying the clothes that Hathaway was wearing. He drops them on the table up* LC *and is about to return to the alcove when his eye is caught by the group consisting of Belgravia, Jubilee and Miss Adshead. He stares particularly at Miss Adshead. After a moment, he crosses to Miss Adshead, takes hold of her head and twists it round to get a better look*)

MISS ADSHEAD (*startled out of her life*) Oh! (*She jumps up*)
WALDORF (*startled*) Oh! (*He jumps hastily back*)
MISS ADSHEAD (*recovering*) You're not Mr Hathaway . . .
WALDORF (*with a charming smile*) Patent-Pending.

(Miss ADSHEAD *looks curiously at him*)

With a hyphen.
MISS ADSHEAD. I want to speak to Mr Hathaway.
WALDORF. I'm afraid you can't—not at the moment. At least, he can't speak to you.
MISS ADSHEAD (*with a step towards him*) It's extremely urgent.
WALDORF. Perhaps I can handle you? I'm the deputy chairman.
MISS ADSHEAD. Miss Adshead. (*Significantly*) Olux. (*She thrusts out her hand*)
WALDORF (*as though it were a greeting*) Olux! (*He thrusts out his hand, but misses hers*)
MISS ADSHEAD (*explaining*) Olux Lamps. Park Royal. I'm their number one Boffin.
BELGRAVIA. Now we know what it is.
WALDORF. Boffin?
MISS ADSHEAD. Backroom girl. Research. The Double Strength is mine.
WALDORF (*interested*) You have double strength?
MISS ADSHEAD (*a little impatiently*) The U.V. The lamp. Mr Hathaway telephoned. There's been a most unfortunate mistake. What you have here is the T.S. model. Triple Strength! Still in the experimental stage—we couldn't think what we'd done with it. (*She moves* R)
BELGRAVIA. You little know what *we* have.
MISS ADSHEAD. It mustn't be used at any cost. It's intended to produce fertility in mules.
WALDORF. Mules?

ACT III MAN ALIVE 69

Miss Adshead (*enthusiastically*) An obstinate problem for years. Of course, we don't know yet if we've found the answer.
Waldorf. Oh, I'm sure you have. *I* found it excellent. (*He moves* LC)
Miss Adshead (*astonished*) You? You didn't use it on a mule?
Waldorf. No. Just as I am. It made a very big difference to me.
Miss Adshead (*staring at him aghast; faintly*) I should think it—very probably—I can't even imagine. (*She moves to the chaise and sits on it, at the right end*)
Waldorf (*moving and sitting* L *of her on the chaise*) It made quite a difference to Mr Hathaway, too.
Miss Adshead (*horrified*) Mr Hathaway? Has *he* been using it?
Waldorf (*nodding and smiling*) He had the infra red.
Miss Adshead (*anxiously*) And is he still all right?
Waldorf. Oh, he's still all right.

(Fred *enters up* C. *He carries a small order form*)

Fred (*moving to* L *of Waldorf*) Mr Pending, sir?

(Waldorf *nods*)

From the wine department. The manager says you'll have to sign this.
Waldorf (*blandly*) Certainly.

(Fred *hands the form and a pencil to* Waldorf, *who makes a large cross on the form*)

(*To Miss Adshead. Proudly*) The Oakshott showed me how to do that. She's going to teach me how to write words next.
Miss Adshead (*staring*) Oh, how splendid!

(Waldorf *graciously returns the form to* Fred, *who stares in astonishment*)

Fred *exits up* C)

(*She rises hastily*) I really must see Mr Hathaway—immediately.
Waldorf (*rising; enthusiastically*) Oh, yes—you must. (*With a friendly smile*) Won't keep you a moment. (*He pats her cheek*)

(Waldorf *exits purposefully by the alcove up* L)

Belgravia. Don't look now, but I think we're going to have company.

(Miss Adshead *moves up* C *and looks towards the alcove up* L. Waldorf *carries* Hathaway *on from the alcove up* L. Hathaway's *arms stick stiffly out in front of him. He is dressed in a preparatory schoolboy's outfit, scarlet blazer and cap, and grey shorts and stockings. The blazer has white lettering embroidered on the breast pocket. He has an outraged expression on his face.* MISS ADSHEAD *retreats down* R. WALDORF *puts Hathaway down* C)

WALDORF (*to Miss Adshead*) There we are.
HATHAWAY (*in a strangled voice*) Sister—send for Sister.
WALDORF. Looks pretty good, doesn't he?
MISS ADSHEAD (*moving above the chaise; not interested*) Yes, yes, very nice. (*A little impatiently*) Will you be long?
WALDORF (*puzzled*) Long?
MISS ADSHEAD. Dressing the window.

(WALDORF *looks at her, then smiles flirtatiously*)

WALDORF. No time at all. I must just display him to the best advantage. I promised Mr Wembley. (*He swivels Hathaway a little so that he semi-faces Jubilee and Belgravia, and tries Hathaway's arms, head and body in various positions*) He's a little stiff—new this morning, of course. He'll be a lot better when we've had him to pieces a few times. (*He turns one of Hathaway's feet out, puts his hands above his head and tilts his head on one side, in a "ballet" pose*)
HATHAWAY (*outraged*) Pieces? I shall tell the shop shopsteward. It's a criminal action. I'm being made away with.
WALDORF (*looking appraisingly at Hathaway*) Really quite lifelike, isn't he?

(WALDORF *exits by the alcove up* L. MISS ADSHEAD *paces impatiently down* C)

HATHAWAY (*desperately*) Help, whoever you are, help!
BELGRAVIA. Waste of breath—she can't hear you.

(MISS ADSHEAD *paces down* L)

HATHAWAY (*startled*) What! Who said that?
BELGRAVIA. I did. Master Hathaway, I presume?
HATHAWAY. Who the devil are you?
BELGRAVIA. The Belgravia. One of two dozen. Delivered June the fifth, nineteen-fifty-one.
JUBILEE. And I'm the Jubilee. Special model. January the tenth, eighteen-ninety-seven. (*Brightly*) Welcome to window thirteen.
HATHAWAY (*hoping to convince himself*) This is a nightmare I'm having, that's all it is. Look at the way I'm dressed.
BELGRAVIA. And—welcome to your second childhood, too. This one's going to last a lifetime.

(WALDORF *enters by the alcove up* L. *He carries a toy pistol, a small Union Jack and a toy trumpet.* MISS ADSHEAD *turns expectantly towards him*)

WALDORF. These go with it somewhere. (*He moves to* R *of Hathaway*) Shan't be long now.

HATHAWAY (*angrily*) If you dare to touch me again, I shall...

(HATHAWAY *breaks off as* WALDORF *puts the handle of the flag in his mouth*)

BELGRAVIA. Now you know what we go through, every time you have one of those inspirations.

(WALDORF *puts the pistol in Hathaway's right hand and points it at Hathaway's temple, in a suicidal pose*)

Russian roulette, I suppose.
JUBILEE. Oh, no, dear. That would be in Indoor Games.

(WALDORF *takes the pistol from Hathaway and puts it in Hathaway's pocket, then takes the flag from Hathaway's mouth and puts the trumpet in its place.* MISS ADSHEAD *stares in astonishment*)

HATHAWAY. Hear me, for Heaven's sake, hear me.
BELGRAVIA (*lyrically*) Trumpeter, what are you sounding now?
JUBILEE. We had a tableau like that once, of the Battle of Balaclava. It said "See the Light Brigade on the Third Floor. No charge".
WALDORF (*catching Miss Adshead's look*) You don't care for it? (*He puts the flag in Hathaway's left hand*)
MISS ADSHEAD (*looking anxiously at Waldorf*) That lamp must be even stronger than I thought.
WALDORF (*referring to Hathaway's pose*) Perhaps you're right. (*He puts the trumpet to Hathaway's ear*) That's better. (*He speaks down the trumpet*) Hullo. (*He blows down the trumpet*)
HATHAWAY. Oh, wind!

(MISS ADSHEAD *crosses and stands up* R. WALDORF *tries a different position, and finally settles for the flag held in one hand and the trumpet in the other. He steps away to take a final look*)

WALDORF. Quite a credit, I think, to our Men's Tailoring.
BELGRAVIA. All we need now is "Rule Britannia".
WALDORF. Of course, he'll look even better in the White Sale. (*He smiles at Belgravia*) I'm going to put him into lace table mats for that. (*He turns away*)
BELGRAVIA (*delightedly*) Good.

(WALDORF *moves to the table up* LC *and collects a show card*)

HATHAWAY (*aghast*) Table mats! (*Even more aghast*) The White Sale! That's more than a month from now.
JUBILEE (*cheerfully*) That's nothing at all. Wait till you've had fifty-nine years of it, like I have.
BELGRAVIA. That's right—comes the turn of the century you'll still be at it—in and out of London's largest range of second-rate suitings.

HATHAWAY (*indignantly*) How dare you!

(WALDORF *moves to Hathaway with the card*)

What's that?

BELGRAVIA. "Ten and six, complete with spare parts." Very reasonable.

(WALDORF *hooks the show card on Hathaway then moves to the table up* LC *and collects a feather duster*)

HATHAWAY. This is more than flesh and blood can stand.

BELGRAVIA. You should worry—you no longer consist of either.

JUBILEE. The first store chairman to become a dummy. One up to good old Hathaway's.

HATHAWAY (*infuriated*) I am *not* a dummy! I'm a human being.

BELGRAVIA (*dryly*) You want to hear the staff on that point.

(WALDORF *energetically dusts Hathaway, his bare knees, etc.*)

That's another little daily delight you'll get used to.

HATHAWAY. Oh, feathers now.

(WALDORF *finishes dusting and crosses to Miss Adshead*)

WALDORF (*with a gleam in his eye*) All ready now.

MISS ADSHEAD. Can we go, then?

WALDORF (*a little taken aback*) Go?

MISS ADSHEAD (*impatiently*) I thought you were going to take me along.

WALDORF (*puzzled, then brightening*) Oh, you mean to the boozy little old party?

MISS ADSHEAD (*staring*) If you choose to put it that way—yes.

WALDORF. Splendid. (*He thinks of something*) Oh, by the way—would you care for one of these? (*He offers her a handful of the costume jewellery*)

MISS ADSHEAD (*horrified*) Certainly not. Thank you.

WALDORF. Funny. No-one seems to. (*He turns to put the jewellery on the chaise*)

MISS ADSHEAD. You don't leave those lying about?

WALDORF. Don't you? Oh. I know. We'll let *him* look after them. (*He moves to Hathaway and puts the jewellery into the side pocket of Hathaway's blazer*) There we are. Now then—(*he picks up Hathaway's clothes*) I'll just put his things in Remnants—and then, Miss Adshead, we'll start things popping. Follow me.

(WALDORF *exits blithely with* MISS ADSHEAD *up* C)

HATHAWAY (*desperately*) Waldorf! Woman! I will not *stand* for this.

BELGRAVIA. You can't do anything else but.

JUBILEE (*cheerfully*) Not till somebody sits you down.
HATHAWAY (*viciously*) If I ever come out of this alive, I shall personally see to it that every dummy in the store is dismembered and disposed of.
JUBILEE. Now, Mr Hathaway, I'm afraid that's being childish.
HATHAWAY (*furiously*) Silence! You horrid old tot!
JUBILEE (*outraged*) Old *tot!* Well, you're not such a young tot yourself. I remember your dear papa bringing you round the store—you stole some bull's-eyes in Confectionery.
HATHAWAY (*taken aback*) What! But no-one ever saw that.
BELGRAVIA. The things *we* see, you'd be surprised. Well done, Jubilee, you hit the target with the bull's-eyes.
HATHAWAY. Well, hang it, I was only a little boy at the time.
BELGRAVIA. Yes. A most obnoxious one, I should imagine. And speaking of pinching things, Mr Hathaway, what about that girl's behind? Behind the fitting-room, in Model Gowns?
HATHAWAY (*still more dismayed*) That—that was just a momentary impulse, nothing more.
BELGRAVIA. Momentary or not, you were quite a big boy, then, weren't you? It was the day before yesterday to be precise.
JUBILEE. Oh dear, Belgravia—how right you've always been. Feet of clay.
BELGRAVIA. Yes. In more ways, now, than one.

(MISS YATES *enters up* C. *She carries a parasol and moves to Belgravia*)

HATHAWAY. Miss Yates! Please! (*Angrily*) Miss Yates! (*Pitifully*) Miss Yates—I'll never speak harshly again.
JUBILEE. There are words we speak in anger,
There are words that gaily fall,
But the words that go unanswered
Are the saddest words of all.

(MISS YATES *opens the parasol and puts it in Belgravia's left hand*)

HATHAWAY. Oh, for God's sake!

(WEMBLEY, *very agitated, enters up* C *and moves below the chaise*)

WEMBLEY. Mr Hathaway. Still not here?
HATHAWAY (*exasperated*) Of course I'm here, man.
MISS YATES. I haven't a notion where he is.
WEMBLEY (*pacing agitatedly down* R) If he doesn't make an appearance soon, it'll be the end of Hathaway's, I can tell you that. (*He paces below Hathaway to* LC) Oh, what can have happened to him?
MISS YATES (*cheerfully*) Perhaps somebody's murdered him at last.

WEMBLEY (*crossing to* R *of Hathaway and leaning on him*) It may be a joke to you, Miss Yates, but it isn't to me.
HATHAWAY (*frantically*) What d'you think it is to *me!*

(WEMBLEY *turns and looks at Hathaway*)

WEMBLEY (*in an exasperated tone*) Look at that! (*He snatches the flag, crosses and puts it on the dressing-table*)
HATHAWAY (*calling desperately*) Wembley! Why can't the fool see me?
JUBILEE. They don't often look at our faces.
BELGRAVIA. Why should they? They don't even look much when we're stripped to the buff.
HATHAWAY (*aghast*) The buff?
BELGRAVIA (*calmly*) You wait and see. Just a giggle or two, perhaps, from one of the juniors.
JUBILEE. After all, what we have on is all they care about.
HATHAWAY (*indignantly*) Yes—and what *have* I got on!
BELGRAVIA. Well, you asked for something preparatory for the coming season.

(DAPHNE *enters up* C. *Her manner is a little excited. She carries a paper windmill*)

DAPHNE. Miss Yates! (*She moves down* L) I don't know *what's* happening in Maternity. I just saw the under buyer with a bottle of champagne—*swigging* from it.

(MISS YATES *moves between Belgravia and Jubilee and makes adjustments to Belgravia.* DAPHNE *kneels by Jubilee and attaches the paper windmill to the handlebars of the tricycle*)

BELGRAVIA. Perhaps they've had a christening there at last.
HATHAWAY (*plaintively*) Miss Jameson . . .
WEMBLEY. It's not only in Maternity—it's all over the store.

(OAKSHOTT *enters breathlessly up* C)

OAKSHOTT. I say! Have you heard the latest? Free champagne in every department. (*She moves above the chaise*) Staff *and* customers.
WEMBLEY (*to Miss Yates*) What did I tell you?

(OAKSHOTT *moves to Wembley*)

HATHAWAY (*groaning*) This is ruin. Utter ruin.
OAKSHOTT (*moving to* R *of Hathaway*) There's chaos in Glass and China. They're filling *everything*.
HATHAWAY (*despairingly*) Oakshott . . .
OAKSHOTT (*leaning on Hathaway*) And what they're drinking from in some of the other departments—you wouldn't believe.
MISS YATES. But why? What does it mean?
DAPHNE. Is it a stunt? For the Sale?

WEMBLEY (*acidly*) You may well ask. Ordered by our new deputy chairman, if you please.
HATHAWAY (*vehemently*) He's not. He's nothing of the kind.
MISS YATES (*mystified*) Deputy chairman?

(WALDORF *enters up* C. *He is now immaculately dressed in morning coat and striped trousers, and has a carnation in his buttonhole. He carries a bottle of champagne.* WEMBLEY, *by way of answer, looks acidly in Waldorf's direction.* MISS YATES *and* OAKSHOTT *gape admiringly at Waldorf*)

WALDORF (*moving to the dressing-table; blithely*) I think I'm going to need my carrier bag.
DAPHNE (*staring at him*) Waldorf! (*To Miss Yates and Oakshott*) Doesn't he look wonderful! (*She moves above the chaise*)

(MISS YATES *moves above the chaise.* WALDORF *puts the bottle of champagne on the dressing-table*)

BELGRAVIA (*bitterly*) Oh, hell!
WALDORF. I feel wonderful! I had a bottle of champagne and another rum sundae. (*He picks up his carrier bag and moves below the chaise*)

(OAKSHOTT *moves to* L *of Waldorf*)

HATHAWAY. Waldorf, I *demand* that you point me out immediately.
WEMBLEY (*to Waldorf*) May I ask where you obtained that outfit?
HATHAWAY (*exasperated*) Never mind the outfit, you damn fool!
WALDORF. I saw it on my way to the wine department. It said, "for the most important day of your life" so I thought I'd put it on. (*He glances around*) Champagne for everybody?
WEMBLEY (*sharply*) Certainly not. And furthermore, it's gone twelve. If this blind isn't up soon, Mr Hathaway will really have something to say.
HATHAWAY (*frantically*) Don't you *dare* pull that blind up!

(MISS YATES *is finishing up.* DAPHNE *is making a list of items on a notepad*)

WALDORF (*blandly*) Well, that won't take a moment. (*He hands the carrier bag to Wembley*) Would you mind? (*He crosses towards the blind pulley. To Wembley*) I hope you found him quite satisfactory?
HATHAWAY. I'm not at all satisfactory.
WEMBLEY. Found who? (*He puts the carrier bag on the stool*)
WALDORF. The new dummy. (*He puts the trumpet to Hathaway's mouth, held with both hands*)
WEMBLEY (*impatiently*) Oh, yes, yes.
HATHAWAY (*hoarsely*) No—no—I'll be a public spectacle!
BELGRAVIA. You've been a public nuisance for years.

HATHAWAY (*in despair; moaning*) No—no—Wemshott—Oakley—Miss Yateson . . .
WALDORF. Up she goes then. (*He starts to raise the "blind"*)
HATHAWAY (*frantically*) No, no, down she stays!

(GEORGE *hurries in up* C. *He is in a state of considerable agitation, which increases a hundred-fold when he sees Hathaway. He hurries to Waldorf, draws him away from the pulley, and the "blind" drops*)

(*Almost at his last gasp*) Ingle!
WALDORF (*severely*) Ingle—please.
GEORGE (*crossing to* L *of Hathaway; aghast*) You can't put *him* in the window!
WALDORF. Why not?
WEMBLEY. Put who?
GEORGE (*incredulously*) Haven't you noticed? (*He stares at Hathaway*) Who on earth put him into these?
WALDORF (*moving* LC) I did. Suit him nicely, don't they?
WEMBLEY (*exasperatedly*) What are you talking about?
GEORGE (*indicating Hathaway*) It's him. The old . . . It's Mr Hathaway.

(*The others all move down and look at Hathaway*)

WEMBLEY. Ingle—are you out of your senses? (*He glances at Hathaway, then starts violently. His voice trails away and he goggles. Faintly*) Or am I? (*He moves* RC)

(MISS YATES, DAPHNE *and* OAKSHOTT *move above the chaise*)

MISS YATES (*astounded*) Good heavens alive!
BELGRAVIA. Just the reverse.
WEMBLEY (*ominously*) Ingle—is this your doing, too?
GEORGE (*unhappily*) It was the infra red. We were using it to try and—(*he glances uncomfortably at Waldorf*) well, we were using it—and that's what happened.

(DAPHNE *looks angrily at George, realizing what happened.* WEMBLEY *moves to* R *of Hathaway, and speaks as to an invalid*)

WEMBLEY. Mr Hathaway—it's Wembley speaking—Gent's Outfitting. (*Getting no response, he tentatively pats Hathaway's hand*)
WALDORF (*helpfully*) He takes to pieces—shall I show you? (*He puts his hand to Hathaway's head*)
WEMBLEY (*agitatedly*) Certainly not! Stand away, there! (*In distress*) Oh, what *are* we going to do?
WALDORF (*brightly*) Champagne, everyone? (*He crosses to the dressing-table*)

(WEMBLEY *agitatedly tries to massage Hathaway's hands*)

WEMBLEY. Mr Hathaway, can't you feel *anything*? (*He gingerly*

ACT III   MAN ALIVE   77

slaps Hathaway's face, then tries again, a little harder. Nothing happens. He moves behind Hathaway and shakes him, then moves to L *of him*)
    OAKSHOTT. Go on, give him a real clip, while you're about it.

    (WEMBLEY, *pained, glances at Oakshott. There is a sudden "pop" as* WALDORF *opens the champagne*. WEMBLEY, *startled and alarmed, looks in a panic at Hathaway, then looks exasperatedly at Waldorf as he sees the source of the noise.* WALDORF *pours the champagne into the vases, powder bowl, etc., on the dressing-table.* WEMBLEY *turns, to try again with Hathaway*)

    GEORGE. It's no use, Mr Wembley, I've tried everything.
    WALDORF. Try this. (*He hands round the champagne*)

    (GEORGE *glares at* WALDORF, *who, unperturbed, turns to offer drinks to Miss Yates and Oakshott*)

    OAKSHOTT (*looking at Hathaway*) Perhaps a good rub down from Sister would get his circulation going.
    MISS YATES. Or a hot bath. (*She accepts a drink from Waldorf*) There is one through there. (*She points* R)
    HATHAWAY (*outraged*) I will not take a bath in the window.

    (DAPHNE *accepts a drink from* WALDORF, *who turns away towards the dressing-table*)

    WEMBLEY (*dubiously*) No water laid on. We might take him home in a van.
    BELGRAVIA. Deliveries daily—all parts of London.
    HATHAWAY (*outraged*) I will *not* go home in a van!
    WEMBLEY (*hopefully*) Perhaps we'd better do that. It should have *some* effect.

    (WALDORF *pours some champagne into the tooth glass*)

    GEORGE (*to Wembley*) And suppose he melts altogether—then what?
    WEMBLEY (*deflated*) I hadn't thought of that.

    (WALDORF *gives the tooth glass to* WEMBLEY, *who looks at it almost abstractedly, then, as though it might solve the problem, takes a big gulp of champagne. The others drink.* WALDORF *returns to the dressing-table, picks up the bottle and moves to Hathaway*)

    BELGRAVIA. I can see the headline in the *Draper's Gazette*—"Hathaway goes into Liquidation".

    (WALDORF *puts a dab of champagne behind Hathaway's ears*)

    GEORGE (*crossing to* R *of Hathaway*) There's only one chance—that's the U.V.

    (WALDORF *refills the drinks*)

But it's gone back. And they won't send it back again—not without—(*he indicates* HATHAWAY) his personal instructions.

WEMBLEY (*with determination*) I'll have a word with them. (*He moves towards the exit up* C)

GEORGE. No good—I had words for half an hour.

(WEMBLEY *stops and turns*)

They said they'd have to have it from his own lips.

JUBILEE. "If those lips could only speak". That was all the rage in eighteen-ninety-seven.

GEORGE (*miserably*) He told them he never wanted to see another of their lamps in his life.

BELGRAVIA. Famous last words.

(GEORGE *and* WEMBLEY *look helplessly at each other*)

DAPHNE (*suddenly, with the courage of champagne*) If you ask me, it serves him absolutely right. (*She moves down* R)

GEORGE (*aghast*) Daphne! What do you mean?

DAPHNE (*accusingly*) You know what I mean. (*She glares at* HATHAWAY *and takes a pace towards him*) The old horror!

(GEORGE *puts his hands over* HATHAWAY'S *ears*)

HATHAWAY (*grimly*) I heard.

MISS YATES (*horrified*) Daphne! (*She glances round involuntarily at* HATHAWAY, *but of course there is no visible reaction. As she realizes this, her face lights up, she giggles and sips her drink*)

(WALDORF *moves down* R)

As a matter of fact, I entirely agree. (*She giggles*)

OAKSHOTT (*after a good gulp of champagne*) Hear jolly well hear! (*She drinks*)

WEMBLEY (*scandalized*) Oakshott! (*Angrily*) This is *disgraceful!* Just because Mr Hathaway is not in a position to . . . (*He gives a slight giggle and hastily pulls himself together*) Just because poor Mr Hathaway has met with . . . (*He glances at* HATHAWAY, *giggles and takes a drink*) Just because . . . (*He gives way to helpless laughter and sits on the tricycle handlebars*)

(MISS YATES, OAKSHOTT *and* DAPHNE *laugh heartily.* GEORGE *looks agonized*)

GEORGE. It's nothing to laugh at—nothing at all.

HATHAWAY (*furiously*) You're fired—every one of you—*fired!*

WEMBLEY (*delightedly*) For the first time in his life—(*he rises*) he has to stand there and let us do the talking. (*He drapes his arm in a carefree manner over* HATHAWAY'S *shoulder*) Pompous old idiot!

BELGRAVIA. The Store with the Team Spirit.

JUBILEE. I can't remember anything like it—since the Suffragettes.

OAKSHOTT (*raising her glass to Waldorf*) Here's to good old Wal!
DAPHNE }
MISS YATES } (*together*) Hear, hear!
WEMBLEY }
WALDORF (*good-naturedly*) Hear jolly well hear!

(*Amid laughter, they all drink.* WEMBLEY *finishes his drink*)

WEMBLEY (*flushed with wine*) Same again all round?

(*There are murmurs of approval.* WEMBLEY *crosses to the dressing-table but finds the bottle is empty*)

WALDORF. Same again all gone.
WEMBLEY. Don't you worry. Leave it to me. (*He moves purposefully to the exit up* C)
OAKSHOTT. Here's to good old Wem!

(WEMBLEY *exits up* C. *The sound of voices off can be heard cheerfully singing a popular song*)

DAPHNE (*excitedly*) Hark at them out there.
OAKSHOTT. That's nothing—up in Gramophones, they're having square dances. (*She dances a couple of steps*)

(WALDORF *moves to Oakshott and dances with her.* MISS YATES *and* DAPHNE *dance together for a few moments*)

MISS YATES. If this is going to be a real party—(*she indicates Belgravia and Jubilee*) we'd better move these.
OAKSHOTT. Come on, Wal—Daph—lend a hand.

(OAKSHOTT *and* MISS YATES *carry* BELGRAVIA *off by the alcove up* L)

BELGRAVIA (*as she goes*) I'm beginning to know this window backwards.
JUBILEE. Oh dear, now I'm going to miss an orgy.

(WALDORF *propels* JUBILEE *out through the exit up* C.
DAPHNE *exits by the alcove up* L. GEORGE *glances around then speaks urgently to Hathaway*)

GEORGE. I've got it, Mr Hathaway. If they won't send the lamp back to you, I'm going to take you to the lamp. Wait here a minute, sir.

(GEORGE *dashes into the alcove up* L. *The heart-beat sound is heard*)

HATHAWAY. Bang bang—bang bang. (*He groans*) Oh, God—what's happening to me now?

(*The* DOORMAN *enters up* C.
GEORGE *dashes in from the alcove up* L, *with the dust sheet*)

GEORGE (*as he sees the Doorman*) Pat—thank heaven. (*He hurries*

to Hathaway *and throws the dust sheet over him*) Give me a hand with this, will you?
DOORMAN. Where to? Stockroom?
GEORGE. No, no—taxi.
DOORMAN (*staring a little*) Taxi? (*He shrugs and takes hold of the sheeted Hathaway, tilting him sharply*)

(GEORGE *and the* DOORMAN *drag Hathaway towards the exit up* C.
MISS ADSHEAD *enters up* C. *She carries a glass half-full of champagne and has a gay air*)

(*To Miss Adshead*) Sorry, madam—not a sign of him.

(GEORGE *and the* DOORMAN *exit with* HATHAWAY *up* C. *The heart-beat sound ceases*)

MISS ADSHEAD (*cheerfully*) Couldn't matter less. (*She sings "Shake, Rattle and Roll" and jives below the chaise*)

(MISS YATES, OAKSHOTT *and* DAPHNE *enter gaily by the alcove up* L, *chattering. They break off as they see Miss Adshead*)

Good morning. (*With a friendly air*) Adshead. Olux. Cheers! (*She drinks to them*) Came here to see Mr Hathaway and ran into the widow Clicquot instead. (*She laughs, finishes her drink, puts her glass on the table* C *and sits on the chaise*) Ah, well—had a fascinating time, I must say. (*She takes from her pocket a scarf identical with the other three presented by Waldorf. It is folded, and she opens it out*)

(*The others stare at the scarf, each of them filled with dismay*)

MISS YATES (*dryly*) So I see.

(*The others group round the chaise*)

MISS ADSHEAD (*unconscious of her tone*) I beg your pardon?
MISS YATES (*pulling herself together*) That's a very attractive scarf. Did you buy it in the Sale?
MISS ADSHEAD (*putting the scarf around her neck*) Didn't buy it at all. Present from the deputy chairman. What a specimen he is. (*She sings*) "See you later, Alligator . . ." Brings out the colour of my eyes, doesn't it?
OAKSHOTT (*huskily*) Perfectly.

(MISS ADSHEAD *smiles gaily, rises, crosses to the dressing-table and looks in the mirror*)

DAPHNE (*in a dead voice*) Those scarves—bring out almost anything.

(MISS BUTTERWORTH *enters up* C. *She wheels on a cocktail trolley, liberally loaded with glasses and bottles of champagne. She, too, is wearing one of the scarves, and her manner is gayer than ever*)

ACT III MAN ALIVE 81

Miss Butterworth (*wheeling the trolley down* L) Wow! Did I have to guard this with my life! (*She rearranges her scarf*)

(Miss Yates, Oakshott *and* Daphne *stare at the scarf*)

By the way—if anyone sees Mr Hathaway—lunch today at the Town Hall—the Police Commissioner's coming at one, to pick him up.

Miss Adshead (*crossing to* C) Well—better get back to the lab. (*She pauses momentarily, tempted, as she sees the trolley, then pulls herself together*) Yes, suppose I'd better. (*She moves to the exit up* C, *then stops and turns*) When you do see Mr Hathaway—might just tell him one thing. About the U.V. we don't know yet how permanent the benefits are likely to be. At present it looks as if the effect is inclined to wear off a little too soon. (*With a cheery smile*) Still, we're hoping with the mules, it'll be long enough. Good-bye.

(Miss Adshead *exits up* C)

Miss Yates. I can't think what the assistants at the scarf counter can be doing.

Oakshott (*gloomily*) Wearing them, too, I suppose.

Daphne. I hope they strangle themselves.

(*There is a "pop" as* Miss Butterworth *opens a bottle of champagne.* Waldorf *enters up* C. Miss Butterworth *pours the champagne*)

Waldorf (*crossing to Miss Butterworth; with a friendly smile*) Not too late, am I? (*He takes a glass of champagne*) I saw a lift full of women. "To hold eighteen", it said. But I only had time to hold one or two.

Miss Butterworth. Bubbly one and all?

(Waldorf, *with a friendly smile, turns to the others*)

Miss Yates (*with sudden determination*) Yes—why not? (*With a reproachful look at Waldorf she crosses to the trolley and takes a glass of champagne*)

Oakshott (*grimly*) I can do with it. (*She crosses to the trolley and takes a glass of champagne*)

Daphne (*with a little sob*) I don't think I can do without it. (*She crosses to the trolley and takes a glass of champagne*)

(Waldorf *is left standing* C, *a little forlorn*)

Miss Yates (*bitterly*) Men—they're all alike. Even brand new ones.

Oakshott. It's the same with everything, these days. Quantity first, quality nowhere.

Daphne. Perhaps George was right, after all.

WALDORF (*brightening*)   Well, I think I'll go up and do with something on the third floor. There's a very nice department up there—"Girls—All Sizes".

(WALDORF *smiles and exits up* C)

MISS BUTTERWORTH (*crossing to the chaise*)   He's a bit of a genius, all the same. You should see the figures for the last three hours. Sales are going sky high. (*She raises her glass*) Here's to a slap happy New Year. (*She drinks*)

MISS YATES
DAPHNE } (*together; responding miserably*)   Happy New Year!
OAKSHOTT

(GEORGE, *in a state of alarm, runs in up* C)

GEORGE (*moving down* C)   Look out, everyone, he's coming!
MISS YATES.   What!
OAKSHOTT.   Who?
GEORGE.   Mr Hathaway. Shoved him in a taxi—off we go and he comes to. Whew! Is he on the rampage!

(MISS YATES, OAKSHOTT *and* DAPHNE *hastily dispose of their glasses.*
   HATHAWAY *bustles in up* C. *He is still in his schoolboy outfit*)

HATHAWAY (*moving* C; *angrily*)   What's the meaning of it, that's what I want to know? What in Heaven's name are they *doing* out there! And what was I doing in a taxi—*horizontal?*
MISS BUTTERWORTH (*staring and laughing*)   Mr Hathaway! Is it a fancy dress party, now?
HATHAWAY (*enraged*)   Fancy dress?
GEORGE (*moving to* L *of Hathaway*)   Just take it easy, sir—your things must be in here somewhere.
HATHAWAY.   My things? What are you talking about? What's going on here? Miss Butterworth . . .
MISS BUTTERWORTH (*hastily*)   I think I'm wanted up in the office.

(MISS BUTTERWORTH *exits hurriedly up* C)

HATHAWAY.   Oakshott—Miss Yates . . .
MISS YATES.   Well—it's a little hard to explain . . .
HATHAWAY.   I should say it is. This window—why isn't it dressed by now? It must be well after nine. What time is it?
GEORGE (*moving above Hathaway to* R *of him*)   It's nearly one, sir.
HATHAWAY.   Nearly what? (*He feels for his waistcoat pocket, to get out his watch. Agitatedly*) My waistcoat—what's happened to it? My watch—it's been pick-pocketed. I've been . . . (*He suddenly discovers how he is dressed*) This isn't my business suit. (*He looks at the pocket of the blazer*) St Timothy's First Eleven. Nonsense! I was at

Bedales. What in the name of Heaven . . . ? (*He sees his shorts*) Ingle—have I been running?
  GEORGE. Only from the taxi, sir.
  HATHAWAY (*turning in confusion*) Oakshott—Miss Yates—explain myself.
  MISS YATES. Don't you remember, Mr Hathaway?
  HATHAWAY. Remember? Remember what?

(*The others all exchange relieved glances*)

Come, come now—all of you—what's up? I want to know without delay.
  GEORGE. I think, sir—perhaps you've had some sort of a turn. You're not yourself, sir—anyone can see that. I mean, look what you've got on. And then, in that taxi, horizontal.
  MISS YATES. Overwork, Mr Hathaway—that's what it is.
  HATHAWAY (*in distress*) You mean—I put myself in these?
  OAKSHOTT. Well, who else would, sir—would they? (*Cheerfully*) Nothing at all, really—just a complete nervous breakdown—you'll be right as rain in a year or two.
  HATHAWAY (*in dismay*) Breakdown? You mean—out there—all those people cutting capers—I was just seeing things?

(*The sound of "Auld Lang Syne" sung loudly is heard off*)

No—no—I couldn't have been. Listen to it.
  GEORGE. I can't hear anything.
  HATHAWAY. You can't?

(GEORGE *shakes his head. The others hasten to do the same*)

  OAKSHOTT. Singing in the ears—that's a sure sign, that is.
  HATHAWAY (*in deep distress*) Oh, Merthyr Tydfil!

(WEMBLEY *enters gaily up* C. *He carries a case of champagne.* GEORGE *moves* RC)

  WEMBLEY (*moving to* R *of Hathaway*) Here we are! A dozen of the best in stock.

(HATHAWAY *stares at Wembley*)

Just look at the old blighter's face! Did you ever see anything like it?
  HATHAWAY (*with a step towards Wembley*) Wembley!

(WEMBLEY *nearly jumps out of his skin*)

  WEMBLEY. Oh! Oh, Mr Hathaway—we're so glad to see you back, sir. (*He puts the case into Hathaway's arms*) With the compliments of the staff.

HATHAWAY (*staring at the case*) Champagne? I suppose this is all in my imagination, too?

(*They are all momentarily stumped, then* DAPHNE *suddenly runs to the chair up* C)

DAPHNE. Oh, no, Mr Hathaway—that's part of the window display.
HATHAWAY. It's what?

(GEORGE *takes the champagne from Hathaway and puts it beside the chaise*)

DAPHNE (*picking up the wedding dress and veil*) Don't you remember, sir? It's to go with these. (*She moves to the trolley*) And this. Isn't it, Mr Wembley?
WEMBLEY (*swallowing*) Yes, that's right.
MISS YATES (*to Hathaway*) Of course. You ordered it yourself.
HATHAWAY (*utterly shaken*) I did?

(*They all nod.*
  MISS YATES *gestures quickly to* DAPHNE *and they both exit by the alcove up* L, *taking the dress and veil with them*)

(*To George*) You must be right, Ingle—I have had some sort of a turn.
GEORGE. I don't know what you've done with your things, sir.
WEMBLEY. We'll get you something off the peg, Mr Hathaway.

(WEMBLEY *and* GEORGE *exit by the alcove up* L)

HATHAWAY. My things—that's nothing. The question is— what have I done with the last three hours?

(MISS BUTTERWORTH *enters dramatically up* C *and moves to* R *of Hathaway*)

MISS BUTTERWORTH. Mr Hathaway—there's two wild women demanding to see you.
HATHAWAY. Two what?
MISS BUTTERWORTH. Customers. They say someone pinched them in a lift.
HATHAWAY. Pinched them where?
MISS BUTTERWORTH. Between the basement and the first floor.
HATHAWAY (*aghast*) Oh, Great Scott, what a breakdown! (*Frantically*) Oakshott—Miss Butterworth—keep them out of here —offer compensation—anything. (*He urges them towards the exit up* C)
OAKSHOTT. They may prefer a charge.
HATHAWAY (*automatically*) All right, then—open an account.

(*Aghast, as he realizes*) Charge! They wouldn't do that, would they? (*He moves down* L)

(*The* DOORMAN *enters up* C)

DOORMAN (*moving to* R *of Miss Butterworth*) Oh—if you please, Miss, the Commissioner of Police is here—to pick up Mr Hathaway.

HATHAWAY (*appalled*) What! Oh, retribution! (*He hides* L *of the trolley*)

MISS BUTTERWORTH (*to the Doorman*) All right—I'll send him in.

(MISS BUTTERWORTH *and* OAKSHOTT *exit up* C)

HATHAWAY (*agitatedly*) No, no. (*He moves* LC) Doorman, you must divert him—quickly.

DOORMAN. Now then, Sonny—you can't lark about in here.

HATHAWAY (*outraged*) Sonny!

DOORMAN. Come on, now—hop it.

HATHAWAY. How *dare* you! (*He crosses to* RC) You must be intoxicated.

DOORMAN. No such luck. I haven't had the time. Come on, now—quick march. (*He catches Hathaway by the neck and shorts and marches him towards the exit up* C)

(*The* POLICE COMMISSIONER *enters up* C. *He is a large man in the early sixties, at once jocular and a little terrifying. He is in uniform*)

HATHAWAY. Oh, no!

(*The* DOORMAN *releases Hathaway and exits up* C)

COMMISSIONER (*jocularly*) Well, young man, what have *you* been up to?

HATHAWAY (*piteously*) If I have, it was just another impulse—I'm not myself at all. (*He moves below the chaise*)

COMMISSIONER (*moving down* C *and staring at Hathaway*) Why—surely—you must be a youngster of Gilbert Hathaway's?

HATHAWAY (*confused*) Youngster . . . (*He realizes and grasps at a straw*) Oh—yes—why not?

COMMISSIONER. Home for the hols, eh? Is that about it?

HATHAWAY. Yes—that's about it. Home for the hols. (*He kicks boyishly at the leg of the chaise then moves above it*)

COMMISSIONER (*genially*) Like school, do you?

HATHAWAY. Oh, yes—very educational.

(*The* COMMISSIONER *stares at Hathaway*)

Er—wizard.

COMMISSIONER (*looking at Hathaway's blazer*) What's this—St Timothy's, eh? And where's that, now?

HATHAWAY. Er—Land's End.

COMMISSIONER. Really. I know Land's End very well—don't recall it.

(*They move down* C)

HATHAWAY (*unhappily*) Well—it's not quite at the end. (*Hastily*) Excuse me, sir—I think I have to be off now. I'm going to the circus, with a little chum. (*He skips up* C)
COMMISSIONER (*surprised*) Circus? There isn't one, this year.
HATHAWAY (*taken aback*) Oh. (*Hastily*) Oxford Circus, I meant. Good-bye, sir. (*He touches his cap and starts to go*)
COMMISSIONER (*moving to Hathaway and grabbing him by the arm*) Oh, no, you don't. (*With mock severity*) I'm going to put you under arrest.
HATHAWAY (*aghast*) Arrest?
COMMISSIONER (*leading him down* C) Till your daddy comes. We're going that way—we'll drop you. (*He glances at his wrist-watch*) He can't be very much longer.
HATHAWAY. He could be. Very much.
COMMISSIONER. Ah, well—busy man, I know. Especially today. Lot on his mind, eh?
HATHAWAY (*with feeling*) Yes—quite a lot.
COMMISSIONER (*indicating the chaise*) Now sit down here, young fellow-me-lad, and tell me all about yourself. (*He sits on the chaise*)
HATHAWAY (*sitting* L *of the Commissioner on the chaise; unhappily*) Oh, there's nothing to tell, really.
COMMISSIONER (*genially*) Well—I expect we can extract a few things, little by little. What's your name, to start with?
HATHAWAY. Er—Eric.
COMMISSIONER. And how old is Eric?
HATHAWAY. Fifty-seven. (*Hastily*) Five and seven. Twelve.
COMMISSIONER (*jovially*) Is that how they teach maths at St Timothy's? (*Confidentially*) Well—now I'll tell *you* something. I'm seven.
HATHAWAY (*startled*) Seven?
COMMISSIONER. Six and one. Sixty-one. (*He laughs and slaps Hathaway's back*)

(HATHAWAY *laughs dutifully and is on the point of slapping the Commissioner's back but remembers just in time*)

Twelve, eh? I have a youngster just about your age. (*He slaps Hathaway's bare knees*)

(HATHAWAY *covers his knees with his shorts*)

Tell you what—you can come to the house one afternoon and have a real scrimmage together. Wouldn't that be smashing?
HATHAWAY. Yes, I'm sure it would. Thank you. Thank you very much.
COMMISSIONER. You can play with his white mice, too. Run

right up your sleeve, under your arm and come out at the back of your neck. (*He "walks" a mouse up Hathaway's arm with his hand*)

HATHAWAY (*suppressing a shudder*) Oh—very delightful. (*He rises and moves* L, *shaking his shorts to get rid of the "mouse"*)

COMMISSIONER (*rising*) Come to think of it, I bought a little something in the shop here, to take back to him. (*He takes a box of allsorts from his pocket*) Like one? Liquorice allsorts.

HATHAWAY (*blenching a little*) Oh—no—not before lunch, thank you.

COMMISSIONER (*incredulously*) No? I don't believe that. There isn't a boy in the world would say "no" to liquorice allsorts.

HATHAWAY (*moving to the Commissioner; unhappily*) Isn't there? Oh. Well, just one, sir. (*He dips in the box*)

COMMISSIONER. Supersonic is my boy's word for them. Don't be modest now—take a handful. (*He empties the box into Hathaway's hands*)

HATHAWAY (*despairingly*) Handful.

COMMISSIONER (*looking at him*) Your voice has broken very early, hasn't it?

HATHAWAY (*trying a higher pitch*) Has it? Well, I had a scrimmage or two last year—perhaps I cracked something. (*He tries to get rid of the allsorts, drops three or four, puts the others on the trolley, then goes on to his knees to pick up those on the floor*)

COMMISSIONER (*moving* R) Well, well—fancy old Gilbert Hathaway had a youngster and he never told me about it.

HATHAWAY. Oh, he never tells anyone.

COMMISSIONER. Old rascal—always makes out he's a bachelor.

HATHAWAY (*preoccupied with the allsorts*) So he is. (*He rises*)

COMMISSIONER (*surprised*) He *is?*

HATHAWAY (*hastily*) Er—yes—Bachelor of Domestic Science. University of London. (*Inspired*) He met mummy there. (*He moves* RC)

COMMISSIONER. Where's mummy now, then?

HATHAWAY. In the British Museum. (*Hastily*) She got a job there. After the divorce. She cleans the other mummies.

COMMISSIONER. I see. And how about little brothers and sisters? Are there any of those?

HATHAWAY. Oh, no. No occasion for those.

COMMISSIONER. Only child, eh? Pity. You're looking a little pale, my boy. Something the matter?

HATHAWAY. Oh, no, sir—thank you—it's just the allsorts. (*Hastily*) A little out of sorts, that's all. Bit too supersonic. I think if I had some fresh air . . . If you don't mind, sir. I don't think I'll wait for daddy. (*He hurries towards the exit up* C)

(GEORGE *enters up* C. *He carries a rather loud check suit*)

GEORGE (*to Hathaway; briskly*) Here we are, sir—sorry to keep you waiting . . .

HATHAWAY (*cutting him short*) Thank you . . . (*He snatches the suit*) Yes. That will be all.
GEORGE (*anxious to help*) If you'd just like to slip into it . . .
HATHAWAY. Not now. I'll slip when I want to.
GEORGE. Well—I hope it'll be a good fit, sir.

(*The* COMMISSIONER *stares at the suit*)

HATHAWAY (*impatiently*) Yes, yes—I'm positive. (*He sees the Commissioner staring*) Daddy's letting me have my first long trousers.

(GEORGE *stares at Hathaway.*
WEMBLEY *enters fussily up* C)

WEMBLEY (*moving to* R *of Hathaway*) I'm afraid the check's a little outspoken, sir. We only had a hound's tooth in your size. (*He sees the Commissioner*) Ah—officer—thank heavens you've got here at last. You've been long enough about it.
COMMISSIONER (*bristling*) I beg your pardon?
HATHAWAY (*agitatedly*) Wembley . . .
WEMBLEY (*turning to Hathaway*) That's the police, these days—spend all their time on parking offences, when really criminal crimes are going on right under their noses.
HATHAWAY (*anxiously*) Oh, no—not as close under as that.
COMMISSIONER (*pricking up his ears; sharply*) There's been a crime here?
HATHAWAY (*in sudden realization*) You mean—you didn't know?
WEMBLEY (*to the Commissioner*) A whole counterful of costume jewellery—in broad daylight.
HATHAWAY (*relief coming over him*) Oh—just a little case of shoplifting. (*He indicates the suit*) I think I could slip now.
GEORGE. Certainly, sir—I'll give you a hand, shall I? (*He undoes Hathaway's blazer and starts to whip it off. As he does so, a glittering piece of costume jewellery flies out of the side pocket. Surprised*) Hullo! What's this? (*He picks up the jewellery*) Good heavens above, sir!
HATHAWAY (*staring at the jewellery*) A rhinestone stomacher!
WEMBLEY. That's one of the missing items! How did it come to be in there?
GEORGE (*feeling in the blazer pocket; excitedly*) Look! There's a whole pocketful. (*He takes the remainder of the jewellery from the pocket*) And all sorts, too.
HATHAWAY (*with a glance at the Commissioner; indignantly*) Certainly not—I've disposed of the allsorts.
WEMBLEY. Oh, what a mercy! I'll see them back to Jewellery. Ingle, bring them along.
HATHAWAY. Never mind—I'll take them myself. (*He turns to go*)

COMMISSIONER (*moving quickly and intercepting Hathaway; formidably*) Oh, no, young man—I don't think you will.
HATHAWAY (*moving down* C) I beg your pardon?
COMMISSIONER (*moving to* R *of Hathaway; severely*) Now look at me, my boy, and give me an honest answer. Did you take those things?
HATHAWAY. Take them? (*Aghast*) Oh, good heavens, did I? Well, what if I did?

(*The* COMMISSIONER *advances on* HATHAWAY, *who retreats round the trolley*)

COMMISSIONER (*following Hathaway*) Deplorable in a boy of your age.
HATHAWAY (*moving above the trolley to* LC; *agitatedly*) That's just it. I'm not a boy of your age. Commissioner, dear old chap, please, let me explain...
COMMISSIONER (*following Hathaway round the trolley and standing* L *of him; sharply*) That's enough. Impertinence and familiarity won't help at all.
WEMBLEY (*moving to* R *of Hathaway; indignantly*) No, they certainly won't. Really, officer, I've never heard of such a thing. I shall report you to your superiors.
HATHAWAY (*agitatedly*) Wembley—please—he *has* no superiors—leave this to me.
COMMISSIONER (*to Wembley; forcefully*) No. To *me*. I have the highest regard for Mr Hathaway myself. But his son can expect no special privileges from the police.
WEMBLEY (*looking at Hathaway; bewildered*) His son? He hasn't one.
COMMISSIONER. I should hope not.
HATHAWAY. Oh, of course I haven't.
COMMISSIONER (*to Wembley*) A little late, now, I'm afraid, to disown the relationship. Oh, we see all too much of this kind of thing these days: good family—good school—and then, for no apparent reason, juvenile delinquency. (*To Hathaway*) You're old enough to know better.
HATHAWAY (*frantically*) I am. I do. They're my own things, what does it matter?
COMMISSIONER. It's a shock, I must admit—even to me—a boy of Gilbert Hathaway's...
HATHAWAY. I'm not a boy of anyone's. (*He jumps up and down*) I'm not. I'm not.
COMMISSIONER (*sharply*) Eric! Control yourself.

(HATHAWAY *staggers back into* WEMBLEY'S *arms*)

HATHAWAY (*desperately*) Eric! There's no such thing. I never had a mummy. Oh, Wembley—identify.
WEMBLEY (*to Commissioner*) Of course—it's Mr Hathaway.

COMMISSIONER. Dressed like that? Now really, man—I'm not a child.
HATHAWAY. Nor am I. Oh, tell him, can't you? Ingle . . .
GEORGE (*to the Commissioner*) That's right, sir—it's the boss. It's all my fault, really. You see, what happened . . .
COMMISSIONER. I know just what happened. Oh, I understand your loyalty well enough . . .

(GEORGE *crosses and puts the jewellery on the dressing-table*)

HATHAWAY. You don't understand anything. (*Frantically*) Oh, there must be some way to show you who I am. Perhaps I've something on me . . . (*He puts a hand in his pocket, produces the toy pistol and points it at the Commissioner. Agitatedly*) Oh, no—I beg your pardon. (*He tries to pocket the pistol*)
COMMISSIONER (*deftly taking the pistol from Hathaway*) Oh, no, you don't. (*He looks at the pistol*) It's a worse case than I thought. I'm sorry, my boy—and I'm sorrier still for your father, but Borstal is the only place for you.
HATHAWAY. Borstal!
WEMBLEY. Oh, Mr Hathaway—and after Bedales.
COMMISSIONER (*to Hathaway*) You'd better come with me. (*He moves to Hathaway*)
HATHAWAY (*moving up* C) Oh! No! Please! I've got an appointment. (*Desperately*) No—no—Wembley—Ingle—can't you show him something?
GEORGE (*moving to* R *of Hathaway; with sudden inspiration*) Yes! I can. Look at this. (*He removes Hathaway's cap, revealing his bald head*)

(HATHAWAY *moves below the chaise*)

COMMISSIONER (*staring*) Great Scotland Yard! What a tragedy!

(MISS BUTTERWORTH *enters up* C. *She carries a slip of paper*)

MISS BUTTERWORTH (*moving to* L *of Hathaway*) Oh—I beg your pardon, Mr Hathaway—from Accounts Department—figures for the first three hours. (*She hands the slip of paper to Hathaway*)

(MISS YATES *and* DAPHNE *enter by the alcove up* L)

MISS YATES. Mr Hathaway—we're ready now to finish the window.

(OAKSHOTT *enters up* C *and stands above the chaise*)

OAKSHOTT. It's O.K., Mr Hathaway, there'll be no charge for the lift.
COMMISSIONER (*realization dawning*) Mr Hathaway—(*he moves to* L *of Hathaway*) Gilbert Hathaway, it *is* you.
HATHAWAY. Of course it is—I haven't been myself, that's all.

COMMISSIONER (*goggling at him*) You don't look it. (*He crosses to* L)

(MISS BUTTERWORTH *moves to the exit up* C.
WALDORF *enters up* C, *sees Miss Butterworth and brightens*)

WALDORF. Ah, there you are. I didn't like girls all sizes. You're the size I like. (*He makes a grab at Miss Butterworth*)

(MISS BUTTERWORTH *eludes Waldorf, glances anxiously at Hathaway, then exits up* C. WALDORF *promptly turns to follow her off, but* HATHAWAY, *staring at him in sudden remembrance, restrains him and brings him down* LC)

HATHAWAY (*formidably*) Just a minute. Commissioner, I want to give this thing in charge.
COMMISSIONER (*a little exasperated*) To *me*? At lunch time? What for?
HATHAWAY. I don't know—impersonating a human being.
COMMISSIONER. For *what*? Who is he?
WALDORF (*with a friendly smile*) I'm the deputy chairman.
HATHAWAY. The ex-deputy chairman.
WALDORF (*brightly*) Oh, is that even better? (*To the Commissioner*) I say, whose doorman are you?
COMMISSIONER (*affronted*) Doorman?
HATHAWAY (*to Waldorf; with grim satisfaction*) He is the police.
WALDORF. Oh, really? (*To the Commissioner*) I was coming earlier on, to see your station.
HATHAWAY. Yes—a thousand pities you didn't.
WALDORF (*fingering the Commissioner's badge of rank*) You like costume jewellery, don't you?
COMMISSIONER (*angrily*) Leave that alone!
WALDORF (*brightly*) I'll give you some more. Oh, now where did I put that . . . ? (*He looks around, then crosses to the dressing-table*)
HATHAWAY. Costume jewellery! Was it you took that?
WALDORF. Oh, yes, I took a lot. (*He picks up the jewellery*) And liberties, too, so they told me.
HATHAWAY (*to the Commissioner; triumphantly*) You see! It wasn't me at all. I may have had a turn, but juvenile delinquent, no. Commissioner, do your duty. (*He crosses to Waldorf*) Oh, it's all coming back to me now—the whole thing. You put me into these.

(*The* COMMISSIONER *crosses to Waldorf, snatches the jewellery from him and puts it on the dressing-table*)

You had the infernal impertinence to order champagne all over the store. Inciting all my staff to mutiny.

(WEMBLEY, GEORGE, OAKSHOTT, MISS YATES *and* DAPHNE *exchange anxious glances and turn to go*)

(*To the staff. Sharply*) Stay where you are. (*To Waldorf*) Well, sir, let me tell you this—I'm going to make things hot for you.

WALDORF. Oh, thank goodness for that. I seem to be getting cooler every minute. I don't know if it's the champagne or the rum sundaes. It started up in the Girls' Department. (*Confidentially*) And I learnt a lot of things up there about you, too. From the staff, that is.

HATHAWAY. What sort of things?

WALDORF (*happily*) Oh, things like, "Where's old Nosey Parker?"

(*The staff endeavour, by gesture, to stop Waldorf saying too much*)

HATHAWAY (*taken aback*) What?

WALDORF. And, "Absence makes the heart grow fonder".

HATHAWAY. Oh—oh, I say!

WALDORF. And, "A finger in every pie makes a nasty meal".

HATHAWAY (*distressed*) Oh, how could they? I don't believe they could. You're inventing them.

WALDORF. Oh, no, I couldn't invent anything. I haven't learnt to think yet. I'm going to start that next week. When I've learnt a few more words. (*He smiles in a friendly way*)

HATHAWAY. Oh, dear. Oh, dear me. (*He sits on the chaise at the right end*)

WALDORF. It is tiring, isn't it?

HATHAWAY. What is?

WALDORF. Being a human being. I've only had a few hours of it and I can do with a sit-down already.

(HATHAWAY *moves along the seat to the left end*)

(*He sits* R *of Hathaway on the chaise*) I can't think what it must be like after seventy-five years.

HATHAWAY. Is that what they're saying, too? (*Indignantly*) Fifty-seven.

WALDORF. I don't wonder your temper's worn out. (*He looks at Hathaways's bald head*) Not to mention other places. You ought to take a few hours off, now and then.

HATHAWAY. I only wish I could. How can I? Someone has to look after the business.

WALDORF (*brightly*) Oh, yes, that was another one. "Why doesn't the old fool mind his own business?"

(*The others turn away*)

HATHAWAY. I don't see how I *can* deserve that one. (*He rises and moves* C) Dash it all, it *is* my own business. What's left of it, after this morning. We must be ruined, anyway. Look at the

ACT III   MAN ALIVE   93

figures for the first three hours. (*For the first time, he looks at the slip of paper and starts in surprise*) Well, I'll be jitterbugged!

(*The staff move towards Hathaway*)

STAFF (*ad lib.*) What is it, Mr Hathaway?
HATHAWAY. The figures—why, they're quite astonishing. The last half hour—it's an all time record.

(OAKSHOTT *moves down* R)

WALDORF (*rising*) And you couldn't mind your own business then, could you? You were a dummy.
DAPHNE (*triumphantly*) And Waldorf was the deputy chairman.
WALDORF (*beginning to get rigid*) Yes—deputy—chairman.

(*The transition sound is heard*)

HATHAWAY (*moving to Waldorf*) Waldorf, it seems that I owe you an apology. Any harsh things I may have said were purely in the heat of the moment. Shall we shake on that? (*He takes Waldorf's hand*) Oh, come come, don't stand there like a dummy. (*He suddenly feels Waldorf's rigidity and releases his hand*)

(WALDORF'S *hand stays in mid-air*)

He *is* a dummy! (*He crosses to* L)

(*The transition sound ceases*)

OAKSHOTT (*moving to* R *of Waldorf*) Wal! (*She touches Waldorf's shoulder*)

(WALDORF *starts to fall over.* DAPHNE *rushes to* L *of Waldorf and holds him.* OAKSHOTT *grabs Waldorf's right arm*)

MISS YATES (*half to herself*) That woman—she said it might not be permanent.

(MISS YATES *and* DAPHNE *exit to the alcove up* L)

COMMISSIONER (*to Hathaway; with some heat*) Hathaway—I don't know what you're up to here this morning—but if it's some kind of dubious device to secure publicity, I don't intend to be involved. (*He looks at his watch*) Half-past one. I can't think what the mayor's going to say.

(*The* DOORMAN *enters up* C *and moves to* R *of the Commissioner*)

Still, if you're coming to that lunch—as an adult—I'll wait for five minutes.
DOORMAN. I wouldn't, sir, if I were you.
COMMISSIONER. What?
DOORMAN. There's a policeman after you, sir—for parking.

COMMISSIONER (*outraged*) What! (*He moves to the exit up* C) I'll have that coat off his back, if it's the last thing I do.

(*The* COMMISSIONER *exits up* C.
The DOORMAN *follows him off*)

HATHAWAY (*shattered by everything*) Lunch. I couldn't face lunch. Not after those liquorice allsorts. I think I'll go home and lie down.

WEMBLEY (*scarcely able to believe his ears*) On the first day of the Sale, Mr Hathaway?

HATHAWAY (*as the thought sinks in*) I *have* been overdoing it. Perhaps I've overdone a lot of things. Perhaps a freer hand all round . . . (*To them all*) You never know—this might well be Hathaway's Happiest New Year.

ALL. Oh, Mr Hathaway!

HATHAWAY. I think I'll take a few days off. A few weeks, possibly. (*To Wembley*) Just tell everyone—Team Spirit—all pull together. And when in doubt—do it the Waldorf way.

WEMBLEY (*delightedly*) Certainly, Mr Hathaway.

(WEMBLEY *and* GEORGE *cross to Waldorf and start to move him* C)

HATHAWAY (*anxiously*) Steady with that now. Those things have their feelings, too, you know—just like the rest of us. (*He moves to Waldorf, looks appreciatively at him and gives him a pat*) Waldorf, old man, we're proud to have you in stock.

(HATHAWAY *exits up* C.

MISS YATES *and* DAPHNE *open the curtains of the alcove up* L. BELGRAVIA, *in bridal gown and veil, is revealed in the alcove*)

BELGRAVIA (*dryly*) Here comes the bride.

(MISS YATES *and* DAPHNE *push* BELGRAVIA LC. *Her feet are concealed under the long bridal gown and she simulates movement as though she were on a wheeled stand.* GEORGE *and* WEMBLEY *move* WALDORF *to* R *of Belgravia*)

OAKSHOTT (*crossing to* R *of Waldorf; excitedly*) Did you hear what I heard? Wait till I spread this one through the departments— you'll be able to hear the cheering from here to Swan and Edgars. (*She strokes Waldorf's chest*) Oh, Wal, whatever your faults you were one in a million.

WALDORF (*imitating Oakshott's earlier tone*) That'll do!

(OAKSHOTT *exits up* C)

MISS YATES (*crossing to* R *of Waldorf; enthusiastically*) I second that!

WEMBLEY (*moving to* R *of Miss Yates; happily*) I shall have lunch today in the *Roof-top Rendezvous*—the four course menu. Miss Yates—perhaps you'd care to join me? (*He offers his arm*)

Miss Yates. Mr Wembley—(*with a smile*) perhaps I would. (*She takes Wembley's arm*)
Wembley (*in a kindly tone*) Finish the window, Ingle—then get the blind up.
George. Yes—Mr Wembley. (*He moves the champagne crate up* L *of Belgravia*)
Miss Yates (*gaily*) Back at two, Daphne—or three. Who knows?
Daphne. Yes, Miss Yates.
Belgravia. Mr Hathaway was right. There *is* no such thing as an unsaleable line.

(Miss Yates *and* Wembley *exit up* C. Daphne *arranges the bouquet in Belgravia's left hand, and puts her other hand on Waldorf's left arm, in the customary wedding pose*)

Waldorf. Hullo, Belgravia.
Belgravia (*warmly*) Waldorf. Back from the land of the living.

(Daphne *and* George *complete the job of straightening the window. Neither looks at the other*)

Waldorf (*a little wistfully*) Yes, I don't suppose I'll ever get to the police station now.
Belgravia. There must be a Providence, after all.
Waldorf. If there is, Hathaway's have it. And at half the price.
Belgravia (*rather sadly*) Now you've seen something of the world—something of its women, anyway—I expect you'll spend the rest of your life waiting to go back.
Waldorf. Yes, I expect I will. (*Nostalgically*) Their rum sundaes were wonderful.
Belgravia (*quizzically*) Waldorf, the Conqueror. You're wonderful, too.
George (*moving down* L; *glumly*) Ready?
Daphne (*equally glum*) Yes—all finished.

(George *works the pulley. The "blind" rises and the light of day spreads over the scene. The scattered glasses, champagne bottles, case of champagne and drinks trolley make an effective setting for Belgravia and Waldorf in their wedding pose.* Daphne *moves below the chaise.* George *moves towards the exit up* C)

(*In the old familiar tone*) George. (*She gazes at Waldorf and Belgravia, arm-in-arm*)

(George *stops and turns*)

I will, if you will.
George (*moving to Daphne; his face lighting up*) Daphne! (*He takes her in his arms and kisses her*)
Belgravia. Well, that's cleared *that* up, thank God.

GEORGE (*as they come out of the embrace; ecstatically*) Oh, Daphne! (*He looks out front and gives a startled reaction*) Daphne! The blind's up.

(DAPHNE *looks out front.*
GEORGE *and* DAPHNE, *aghast, run out up* C)

BELGRAVIA. And now I suppose they'll live happily ever after. So will we—till the next time they change the window. Oh, well —it's a long life, but things happen fast sometimes. Look at us. Met this morning, married by lunch-time . . .

(GEORGE *and* DAPHNE *enter up* C, *wheeling* JUBILEE, *who is seated, in baby clothes, in a glossy new perambulator. They wheel her down* C, R *of Waldorf*)

JUBILEE (*brightly*) Hullo again, dears.

(DAPHNE *puts a dummy in Jubilee's mouth*)

BELGRAVIA. Great Scott! *Already!*

The music of the "Wedding March" is heard off. DAPHNE *and* GEORGE *move to the exit up* C, *look at the group* LC, *giggle and exit.* WALDORF, BELGRAVIA *and* JUBILEE *hold their poses as—*

the CURTAIN *falls*

FURNITURE AND PROPERTY LIST

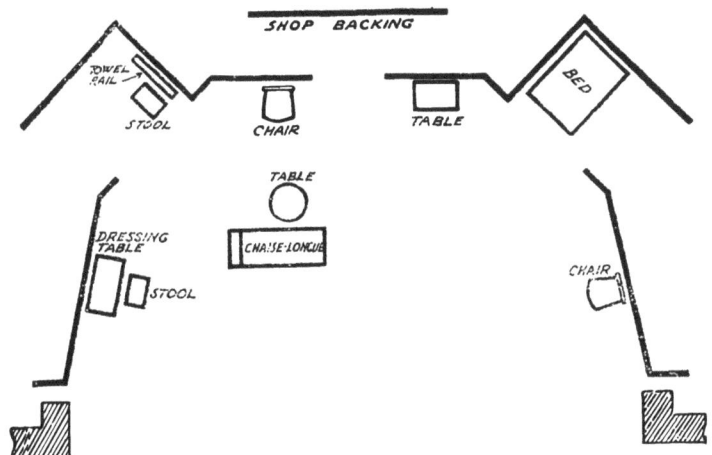

ACT I

On stage: Chaise-longue
Small circular table. *On it:* vase of flowers
Small table (up LC) *On it:* table-lamp, telephone
Bed. *On it:* satin cover
2 upright chairs
Dressing-table. *On it:* vase of flowers, mirror, powder bowls, vases and other suitable dressing
Dressing-table stool
In alcove up R: towel rail, stool
3 pairs electric wall-brackets
Bathroom pendant light
Carpet on floor
3 pairs heavy curtains
Window blind handle and pulley
Batten with fringe

Set: On *chaise:* book
Down L: sun-lamp plugged into skirting
Chair from R of entrance up C to above chaise
On it: boy's dressing-gown

Alcove curtains open
Curtain up C, closed
Light fittings off
Window blind down

Off stage: Feather duster (DAPHNE)
    Notepad and pencil (GEORGE)
    Cardboard box. *In it:* show cards, price tickets, price ticket "9 guineas", price ticket "59/3", show card "WHAT EVERY BOY WANTS", 2 show cards "ULTRA-VIOLET", show card "GLAMOROUS NIGHTS" (GEORGE)
    Show card, bed jacket (DAPHNE)
    Coat, cardigan, dress, hat (OAKSHOTT)
    Pale pink plastic squeaking duck (GEORGE)
    Show card "ROCK BOTTOM 2/6" (MISS YATES)
    Feather duster (WEMBLEY)
    Carrier bag, handbag. *In it:* notebook, pencil (OAKSHOTT)
    Suit and other items of clothing (GEORGE)
    Shirt, socks, shoes, tie, underwear for Waldorf (GEORGE)
    Large aluminium saucepan, whisk (BELGRAVIA)

Personal: MISS YATES: wrist watch
    WEMBLEY: tape measure
    GEORGE: paper and pencil

ACT II

Strike: Chaise-longue
    Saucepan
    Whisk
    Clothing from bed
    Carrier bag from table C

Set: Chair RC to R of exit up C
    On table up LC: price cards, box of pins, tape measure, ink-pad, rubber stamp
    Down L: dust sheet
Alcove curtains open
Curtains up C open
Light fittings on
Window blind down

Off stage: 2 show cards (MISS YATES)
    Showcard "UNREPEATABLE" (MISS YATES)
    Large pink powder puff, loofah, scent spray, inflated rubber bathing ring with a fish's head (DAPHNE)

Blazer, pair of grey flannels, cardigans (GEORGE)
Carrier bag. *In it:* 3 scarves, bunch of roses (WALDORF)
Slip of paper (DOORMAN)

Personal: WALDORF: green National Insurance card
OAKSHOTT: handbag
HATHAWAY: cigar case with cigars

ACT III

Strike: Clothing from bed
Surplus show cards, accessories, etc., from chairs and tables
Dust sheet

Set: Chaise-longue C
Chair up C. *On it:* maternity smock, wedding-dress, bridal veil
On table up LC: show card, feather duster
Alcove curtains closed
Curtains up C open
Light fittings on
Window blind down

Off stage: Clothing (WEMBLEY)
3 straw hats, spray of apple blossom (MISS YATES)
Tricycle with basket and toy rabbit (DAPHNE)
Hathaway's clothes (WALDORF)
Order form and pencil (FRED)
Toy pistol, Union Jack, toy trumpet (WALDORF)
Parasol (MISS YATES)
Paper windmill (DAPHNE)
Bottle of champagne (WALDORF)
Case of champagne (WEMBLEY)
½ glass of champagne (MISS ADSHEAD)
Cocktail trolley. *On it:* glasses, bottles of champagne (MISS BUTTERWORTH)
Loud check suit (GEORGE)
Slip of paper (MISS BUTTERWORTH)
Perambulator (GEORGE and DAPHNE)
Baby's dummy (DAPHNE)

Personal: WALDORF: Hathaway's cigar case with cigars, costume jewellery
DAPHNE: notepad and pencil
MISS ADSHEAD: scarf, watch
MISS BUTTERWORTH: scarf
COMMISSIONER: watch, box of allsorts

LIGHTING PLOT

Property fittings required: sun-lamp with violet and red lamps, switch, flex and plug, 3 pairs electric wall brackets, table-lamp, bathroom pendant (all practical)

Interior. A shop window set as a bedroom. The same scene throughout

THE MAIN ACTING AREA covers the whole stage

THE APPARENT SOURCES OF LIGHT are—wall brackets R, L, up LC and a pendant RC, and daylight presumed to come from the direction of the auditorium

ACT I

To open:	The stage dimly lit Fittings off Flood outside entrance up C, on	
Cue 1	GEORGE switches on lights *Snap in fittings* *Snap in lights to cover*	(Page 2)
Cue 2	GEORGE switches on sun-lamp *Snap in sun-lamp, Ultra Violet circuit*	(Page 13)
Cue 3	GEORGE raises window-blind *Bring in daylight effect*	(Page 15)
Cue 4	GEORGE lowers window blind *Take out daylight effect*	(Page 19)
Cue 5	GEORGE switches off the sun-lamp *Snap out sun-lamp*	(Page 23)

ACT II

To open:	Lights as at the end of the previous Act	
Cue 6	GEORGE switches on the sun-lamp *Snap in sun-lamp, Red circuit*	(Page 52)
Cue 7	DOORMAN unplugs sun-lamp *Snap out sun-lamp*	(Page 59)

ACT III

To open:	Lights as at the end of the previous Act	
Cue 8	GEORGE raises window blind *Bring in daylight effect*	(Page 95)

www.ingramcontent.com/pod-product-compliance
Ingram Content Group UK Ltd.
Pitfield, Milton Keynes, MK11 3LW, UK
UKHW021843210426
5322IPUK00022B/446